WILLIAMS-SONOMA

LONDON

AUTHENTIC RECIPES CELEBRATING THE FOODS OF THE WORLD

Recipes and Text
SYBIL KAPOOR

Photographs
JEAN-BLAISE HALL

General Editor
CHUCK WILLIAMS

Oxmoor
House

CONTENTS

RECIPES

INTRODUCTION

Two thousand years ago, the Romans built an outpost on the river Thames where London's financial district now stands. The population of the settlement was surprisingly international. This character still pervades every aspect of the metropolis, especially its cuisine, a sophisticated fusion of British creativity and global influences.

CULINARY HISTORY

The blueprint of London cooking was first laid down by the Romans. Around 50 C.E. they founded a settlement called Londinium at a ford on the river Thames. At this hub, the Romans began to build a network of roads that soon gave them access to most of Britain and established a port that eventually grew into a center for global trade. The troops occupying the settlement's fortifications came from what is now Syria, Spain, and Italy, as well as other areas within the vast Roman empire. As a result, the population of Londinium was extraordinarily international.

These new residents learned where to harvest native game and fish, and where to obtain local livestock, fruits, and vegetables. The dishes they prepared were Anglo-Roman in style—classic Roman fare such as rabbit stuffed with pine nuts and dates with English ingredients. The upper class seasoned their food with imported delicacies such as olive oil, raisins, wine, pine nuts, and liquamen, a fermented fish sauce.

Little is known of London's culinary tastes after the Roman legions departed in 410 C.E.

There is no doubt, however, that the arrival of William the Conqueror from France in 1066 changed the city's cooking forever. The new king of England insisted on replacing Anglo-Saxon customs and cuisine—rooted in local produce, roasted game, and stewed red meat with herb sauces—with French customs and Norman preferences in food. The roasted and sautéed meat and fowl of Norman cuisine were heavily spiced and served with complicated aromatic sauces containing such ingredients as almonds, ginger, and sugar.

Growing Prosperity

By the thirteenth century, London had developed into a bustling, rich commercial city and a center of political and royal power. This growth in prosperity and sophistication was manifested in the range of dishes prepared by cooks and served primarily at the tables of nobility: distinctly English roasts, grilled meats, and savory pies, and newly adopted French sautés, fricassees, and sauces. Various roasted, fried, and boiled foods were the specialties of cookshops, early

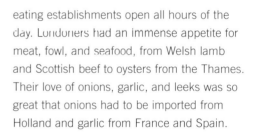

eating establishments open all hours of the day. Londoners had an immense appetite for meat, fowl, and seafood, from Welsh lamb and Scottish beef to oysters from the Thames. Their love of onions, garlic, and leeks was so great that onions had to be imported from Holland and garlic from France and Spain.

Imported Delicacies

Because London was a center of international trade, the city's inhabitants welcomed the arrival of new foods. If nobles desired pigeons stewed with pepper, ginger, and saffron or royal cooks wanted to introduce Italian dishes like macaroni with butter and Parmesan cheese, merchants would import the necessary ingredients. Knowledge of these new recipes and ingredients was spread across the capital by the city's cooks, who belonged to a guild, the Cooks' Company, established in the 1300s.

As competition for the spice trade intensified, Britain sought to import ever larger quantities of spices and seasonings, including sugar. In the sixteenth century, London bakers

began to turn out wonderful spiced and fruited buns such as gingerbread and hot cross buns, and cooks added a variety of spices such as cloves, cinnamon, and fennel to savory meat pies, mince pies, and sweet fruit tarts made with pears or apples. Even the ale houses, early ancestors of the pub (see page 50), spiced their brews by warming ale with ginger, nutmeg, cloves, sugar, and the pulp of tart crab apples to make a drink called lamb's wool. A notable English beverage owes its origins to Britain's robust trade: tea from China was introduced to London in the 1640s by the East India Company, formed to import spices and other goods from the Far East (see page 36).

A Culinary Style Takes Shape

As Britain thrived over the next few centuries, Londoners enjoyed ever better food. The quality of the livestock, seafood, dairy products, and fresh fruits and vegetables brought into the city's vast markets was superb compared with what was sold in many

other European cities. This plentiful and high-quality supply meant that foods did not have to be overcooked or heavily seasoned to mask their lack of taste or freshness. Instead, the city's cooks created simple dishes that celebrated the particular character of a few well-chosen ingredients. Rather than make a complicated, time-consuming French stew with tough and often stringy mutton shanks, cooks could now purchase and roast a tender leg of lamb, then accompany it with home-made red currant jelly. A syllabub of cream with wine and sugar was as delicious as, and took less time to make than, a traditional steamed pudding. Such straightforward dishes, using good-quality ingredients, were regarded as typically English.

This style of cooking reached its zenith during the eighteenth century. At the same time, Londoners continued to dine on an international selection of dishes, just as they had in earlier centuries. Books such as Hannah Glasse's *The Art of Cookery Made Plain and Easy* (1747) and Elizabeth Raffald's

The Experienced English Housewife (1769) included recipes for Indian curry, Turkish mutton, and Portuguese beef. London cooks could buy all the ingredients they needed to make these recipes—spices, dried fruits, chiles, tamarind, olive oils, and vinegars—from specialist grocery shops.

Global Influences

One factor that contributed to this broad and varied palette was the arrival of immigrants from around the world, who came to seek their fortune or flee from difficult circumstances in their native countries. The Italians had a particularly marked impact on the London diet. Not only did they open grocery stores that sold imported foods, but they also established confectionery shops that made and sold sweets such as ices and gelatos. The most famous was Gunter's Tea Shop in Berkeley Square, founded by Domenico Negri in 1757 and named for his British partner, James Gunter, who later operated the shop on his own. At inexpensive Italian restaurants in

Soho and Clerkenwell, avant-garde Londoners dined on roast chicken, imported olives, and brandied cherries, while sipping Marsala.

Culinary Consolidation

The nineteenth century, when London rapidly expanded into a vast metropolis, was a period of culinary consolidation. The Anglo-French style of cooking, combining both French and English recipes, remained the foundation of London cookery. It still dominated the city's tables and was served in many of the grand restaurants and banquet halls. Some of these survive, such as Simpson's Grand Restauratum in the Strand—today called Simpson's-in-the-Strand—founded in 1848, and the Café Royal on Regent Street, dating from 1865. Working Londoners dined on roasted meats, crusty breads, and locally brewed beer in neighborhood restaurants known as ordinaries, or sipped wine while enjoying savory meat and fish pies, hearty stews, and grilled meats at local taverns, the forerunners of wine bars. Street vendors sold steaming bowls of pea soup, creamy baked potatoes, fried fish, and other simple dishes that made up an inexpensive meal.

Yet the dramatic social and economic changes in the twentieth century, brought about in part by two world wars, inevitably impacted London's eating habits. A decreased interest in home cooking and a reliance on processed food led to the city's reputation for bland, overcooked fare. It would take twenty years before Londoners would slowly begin to rediscover fine home cooking.

A New Direction

In the 1970s, Londoners were reintroduced to home cooking and seasonal cuisine, primarily through the writings of Elizabeth David and authors such as Robert Carrier. David extolled the pleasures and rewards of preparing Mediterranean dishes such as Provençal ratatouille and Italian minestrone, and the importance of using proper ingredients like the highest quality extra-virgin olive oil and the freshest basil. Robert Carrier, an American

by birth, introduced Londoners to the concept of glamorous, well-made dishes that drew on influences from around the world, whether a fine French pâté or a Greek moussaka. From these roots, French nouvelle cuisine in particular became popular for its fresh, light approach to cooking.

Also in the 1970s, Londoners began to travel more widely than before on holidays, not only to Spain, Italy, Greece, and other European countries but to other continents. Back at home, they could satisfy their enthusiastic appetite for ethnic foods by dining at the Chinese, Indian, Turkish, and Thai restaurants that were opening up in many neighborhoods throughout London. Unfamiliar ingredients such as Indian garam masala, Chinese lotus roots, and Thai kaffir lime leaves began to appear in specialist shops and delicatessens (see page 42), allowing cooks to prepare ethnic dishes at home. Although many Londoners still had their favorite Anglo-French classics, many others were discovering something new.

CONTEMPORARY CUISINE

London has undergone a remarkable culinary renaissance that emphasizes seasonal foods and ethnic flavors. Sparked by pioneering chefs, the trend has been embraced by home cooks, who eagerly seek out locally grown produce at farmers' markets and artisanal products in the city's many specialty shops.

Most Londoners would have difficulty defining London cuisine, even though many enjoy cooking at home in their leisure time and food is a favorite topic of conversation. Nevertheless, if you were to peek into their kitchens throughout the year, you could gain a sense of the typical London diet.

Seasonal Cuisine

In winter, the preference is for warming dishes such as puréed vegetable soups, fragrant Moroccan tagines with preserved lemons, rich Kashmiri curries, Chinese stir-fries, tender roast leg of lamb with red currant jelly, roast partridge with a classic bread sauce, and buttery fruit pies. Summer is the season for lighter fare; for example, Lebanese-style grilled chicken with herbed yogurt sauce, Mediterranean pastas and salads, barbecued fish and meat, fruit salads, and homemade ice cream. Indian and Chinese takeaway is universally popular, and most Londoners admit to a great fondness for Asian flavors such as soy sauce, chiles, lime leaves, fresh cilantro (coriander), and lemongrass.

Simply prepared English dishes made with ingredients in season are integral to London's cuisine. In spring, it might be an asparagus vinaigrette made with the highly regarded English crop (see page 109) followed by grilled lamb kebabs; in summer, salmon with mayonnaise followed by strawberries and cream. Not only do these foods taste delicious, but they make Londoners feel a connection with the surrounding countryside by reminding them of the changing seasons. Enjoying a steak and wild mushroom pie, roast pheasant, or panfried venison steak followed by an apple and blackberry pie or a pear syllabub in a city restaurant in October or November reinforces the arrival of autumn and conjures up images of long country walks and cozy rural pubs.

The Arrival of Farmers' Markets

The link between town and country has been strengthened in recent years by the increasing number of farmers' markets that have opened across the city. Currently there are close to a dozen farmers' markets scattered throughout London, from Blackheath in the East to Swiss Cottage in the North and Wimbledon in the South. The first farmers' market was opened in Islington in June 1999. All of these markets are dependent on local government and community support to ensure that the market space is reserved and set up on a weekly basis.

Farmers drive in to the London markets from up to a hundred miles (160 kilometers) away, and many specialize in unusual produce such as tatsoi (an Asian green), wild garlic, golden beets (beetroots), and elderberries. Locally made buffalo cheese, smoked trout, and wild game such as mallard duck and partridge can also be found at many of the markets. Many of these foods are

difficult if not impossible to find in super-markets or neighborhood shops, and Londoners take pleasure in being able to talk directly to farmers. Farmers, in turn, give their customers helpful suggestions for preparing unfamiliar produce and foods, and will even forage for certain hard-to-find wild foods such as elderflowers or wild plums upon the request of their customers. Farmers' markets have become so popular in London that more and more open every year.

Reviving Artisanal Food

Coinciding with the popularity of farmers' markets is the revival of small artisanal food shops. Many of these disappeared in the 1970s and 1980s with the proliferation of supermarkets. The quality of the merchandise sold at these shops and the skills of the proprietors were sorely missed by food-loving Londoners, who now relish visiting a butcher who orders goose, pork, or beef directly from their favorite local farms throughout Britain. They can also visit a cheesemonger who

encourages them to sample Stilton from Nottinghamshire, Wigmore from Berkshire, or a selection of local farmhouse Cheddars.

Restaurant Pioneers

The renewed interest in artisanal foods was pioneered by London's chefs, who, frustrated with the limited range of produce, meat, and other items available from restaurant suppliers, began to do their own sourcing of ingredients. Smiths of Smithfield, for example, a lively, informal restaurant adjoining the Smithfield meat market, sought out rare breeds of pigs, sheep, and beef such as Gloucester Old Spot pigs, Tamworth pigs, and Welsh Black beef.

Fergus Henderson, co-owner and head chef of the internationally recognized restaurant St. John, looked for the highest quality ingredients for his "nose to tail" cooking. Many of his renowned specialties are classics that he has revived and updated, such as melt-in-your-mouth roast bone marrow and parsley salad served with sea salt and

country bread, succulent braised oxtail, and tender suckling kid with fennel compote. Restaurants across the ethnic spectrum follow the same approach. Assaggi, a relaxed, stylish Sardinian restaurant on Chepstow Place, for example, imports the finest Sardinian specialties, including wafer-thin *carta da musica* (music-paper bread) and *bottarga* (gray mullet roe).

Since Londoners are familiar with cuisines from around the world, it is a natural step for them to experiment at home by adapting the foods and flavors from other cultures into their recipes. What makes these dishes unique to London is that they adhere to the concept of combining a few well-balanced ingredients. Thus, asparagus might be grilled Italian style and dressed in a Japanese-influenced sesame-soy dressing, or a leg of lamb might be marinated Middle Eastern style with lemon, olive oil, yogurt, cumin, and onion before it is roasted. In either case, the aim remains the same—to create a dish where the best features of each component are enhanced.

DINING OUT

Eating out at a dining mecca owned by a trendsetting chef or at a neighborhood gastropub or ethnic eatery is the essence of social life in London. Residents have more than ten thousand choices, and the city is second only to Paris in its number of Michelin-starred restaurants.

London has an extraordinarily diverse population. A 2003 survey found that the city's schoolchildren speak about three hundred different languages. With people of various nationalities living side by side throughout the city, many neighborhoods have a wide range of ethnic restaurants. Chinese, Indian, and Italian restaurants are as common today in London as its many pubs and wine bars. In most areas, diners have the choice of these and other ethnic restaurants, including Lebanese, Greek, Thai, Japanese, and French. In some neighborhoods, traditional restaurants such as fish and chip shops are becoming harder and harder to find.

Global Cuisine

Ethnic restaurants are among Londoners' favorites, and they usually base their selection on both food and atmosphere. Woodlands on Marylebone Lane, for example, is perfect for a quick, inexpensive vegetarian Indian meal after a day of shopping. Casually dressed diners never feel out of place while sipping mango lassi (a yogurt drink) and eating crisp *dosa* (a South Indian pancake) with vegetable curry and coconut chutney. At the Real Greek in Hoxton Market, groups of friends like to feast on oven-baked giant butter beans, grilled smoked sausages encased in warm rye bread, and Metaxa brandy and sultana ice cream. The

superlative Chinese food of the Michelin-starred Hakkasan on Hanway Place, with its glamorous, dimly lit interior, is often the choice for a special occasion. After savoring enoki mushroom and shrimp (prawn) dumplings and roasted silver cod with Champagne and Chinese honey, diners are ready to visit a nightclub or bar and party until the early hours of the morning.

Simple Masterpieces

Londoners are equally drawn to the myriad restaurants and gastropubs whose cooking may variously be described as Italian, modern British, Mediterranean, or Spanish. Their chefs share an interest in simply prepared, seasonal dishes that highlight the flavor of the core ingredients. A well-known exponent of this approach is the River Café on Rainville Road, where diners can sit outdoors along the Thames and order black truffle risotto, pasta parcels filled with ricotta cheese and wild greens, or baked wild sea bass with treviso. Fino on Charlotte Street, with its interior of red leather and blond wood, serves delectable Spanish tapas such as sautéed clams in sherry and tiger prawns with aioli. Robust Spanish and North African cuisine— grilled eggplant (aubergine) and red pepper salad with flatbread, wood-roasted sardines served with preserved lemons, coriander, and warm potato salad, and yogurt and pistachio cake for dessert—is the specialty at the

critically acclaimed minimalist restaurant Moro located on Exmouth Market.

For formal occasions, Londoners are spoiled by the sheer number of Michelin-starred restaurants scattered across the capital. The majority serve a contemporary London version of Anglo-French or Italian food. Among the best are Gordon Ramsay on Royal Hospital Road and Locanda Locatelli on Seymour Street. Gordon Ramsay's restaurant, with its cool purple interior and quiet staff, has a discreet air, and every dish reflects his restrained, elegant approach. Texture and flavor are perfectly balanced, from the turbot poached in red wine to the celery root (celeriac) risotto to the baked chocolate fondant with orange sorbet. Giorgio Locatelli, the chef behind Locanda Locatelli, epitomizes the current London interpretation of Italian cooking in his light-filled, retro-style restaurant. Using superlative ingredients, he makes such simple, creative Italian dishes as seared scallops with saffron puréed potatoes or an almond fondant pudding with pistachios.

Pub Life

Socializing with colleagues is a common ritual in London, and toward the end of the week, groups of workers head for a nearby pub or wine bar for lunch or an after-work drink. It is hard to walk from one street to the next in London without finding a bar or pub, and part of the enjoyment is discovering a new establishment hidden in a mews or tucked down a narrow passage. The small, wood-paneled Jerusalem Tavern on Britton Street, converted from a house dating to 1720, is particularly popular in winter, when the regulars gather around the fire in the small front parlor and sip the chocolaty winter ale made by St. Peter's Brewery in Suffolk. The Barley Mow on Dorset Street, built in 1791, is frequented mainly by local workers, who sit outside on the wooden benches in good weather and drink Green King IPA or Marston's Pedigree beer. Many pubs offer simple, traditional dishes, such as bangers and mash with gravy or a ploughman's lunch consisting of crusty bread, a wedge of

crumbly cheese, and pickle. Others serve roast chicken, hearty beef pies with mash, and on Sundays, a traditional lunch of roast beef, lamb, or pork, with all the trimmings.

Neighborhood Restaurants

For most Londoners, the neighborhood where they live is an extension of their home. Meeting up with friends at a local gastropub or an ethnic restaurant is a far more informal and relaxed occasion than going farther afield in the city. So regularly do Londoners visit their local pizzeria or Chinese or Indian restaurant that they often know the menus by heart. Relishing the variety available close to their doorstep, Londoners enjoy ordering a superb takeaway—Vietnamese *banh xeo* (chicken and bean sprout pancakes), Turkish grilled kebabs, Chinese squid with black bean sauce, or Indian chicken tikka masala or prawn curry—as much as they love cooking in their own kitchens. Once at home, they can open a bottle of fine wine and await the arrival of friends to enjoy their meal together.

MARKETS

Bustling markets with their winter greens and rosy apples are as much a part of London's heritage as its fine houses and lush parks. Today's farmers' markets, like the older street markets, are a source of good food and lively discourse. They are also re-establishing the ancient link between town and country.

Every day vast quantities of food are trucked, shipped, and flown into London to feed the population of nearly 7.4 million residents. The majority is sold through supermarkets, but a significant quantity goes to wholesale markets: Covent Garden (offering fruits and vegetables as well as flowers), Great Western (selling fresh produce from Asia), Smithfield (carrying a wide range of meat), and Billingsgate (specializing in fish and shellfish). Each market has independent wholesalers who source food from around the world to supply London's hotels, restaurants, and street markets.

Londoners can visit these markets and buy their produce direct, provided they are prepared to get up very early. Since most of the city's chefs have fallen into bed around the time the markets start their daily business, they prefer to rely on specialist restaurant suppliers instead. By 3 A.M. each weekday morning, the wholesale markets are humming with activity. Friendly banter fills the chilly dawn air as fresh produce is unloaded, examined, haggled over, and sold, then reloaded onto trucks and taken to London's street markets or small shops. Some wholesale markets stay open longer to complete the restaurant orders left by chefs at the end of their night shift. Trucks carrying the orders are soon on the road, delivering wild mushrooms or crayfish to restaurants needing them before 9 A.M.

London's wholesale markets are extraordinary places. Only Smithfield remains in the City on its original 1174 site. Its elegant building, dating to 1868, was modeled on the glass-and-iron Crystal Palace of 1851 and has been thoroughly modernized. Billingsgate, founded in 1016, moved from its Roman dock on the Thames to the Docklands farther east in 1982. The romantic seventeenth-century Covent Garden was rehoused in modern facilities in Nine Elms, Battersea, in 1973.

Strolling into the vast halls of modern Billingsgate at around 4 A.M., you will see a staggering array of gleaming fish. One wholesaler might specialize in wild Irish salmon, Scottish lobster, and Dover sole, while his neighbor concentrates on imported exotics such as tropical parrot fish, pomfret, and marlin. Sellers wearing white coats and Wellington boots pick their way purposefully across the wet floors before heading upstairs to complete their paperwork in the offices above the market. Meanwhile, the buyers, often fishmongers themselves, might grab a mug of sweet tea in the building's café before loading up their purchases and heading off to work.

As the wholesale markets wind down, the sellers at the street markets set up their stalls. Street markets have come and gone over the centuries, depending on London's needs. With the rise of supermarkets that buy direct from growers, street markets and independent small shops have declined. All of the market stalls are licensed by their local councils to trade at agreed times. Brixton

Market, for example, sells a glorious array of West Indian and African foods such as casavas, plantains, and callaloo, as well as pigeon peas, catfish, and goat meat. Ridley Road Market in the East End offers a mixture of English, West Indian, and Asian foods. Each market sells ingredients suited to the local population; for instance, Notting Hill's Anglo-Caribbean shops on Portobello Road sell pomelos and chiles; Edgware Road's Anglo-Asian Church Street Market displays Indian beans and white radishes called *mouli;* and Soho's continental Berwick Street offers traditional French and Italian foods such as curly endive and white asparagus. Each costermonger, or street barrow-seller, bellows out prices and tries to lure customers in with lively banter and fine display of produce.

The introduction of farmers' markets and fine food markets has energized London's food scene. In 1999, with the opening of the first farmers' market in Islington, shoppers could meander around the stalls and talk to the people who actually made pork pies from

their own pigs in Somerset or grew their own gooseberries. Since Londoners enjoy dreaming about an idyllic rural life, this direct link to the countryside captured their imaginations. The success of this first market ensured that others would follow—Marylebone, Notting Hill, and Peckham. The markets also created a much-needed outlet for farmers who had been selling to supermarkets through wholesale markets.

London farmers' markets each have different traders, but the atmosphere is much the same, as crowds flock to a car park that has been transformed into a village fête. Tables spill over with fresh Malden oysters, crusty bread, pearly legs of Jacob lambs, Norbury blue cheese, lush bunches of baby turnips, and sprays of wild elderflowers. According to market rules, stall holders can only sell food that has been made, grown, or harvested within a hundred-mile (160-kilometer) radius of London. Thus, English Preserves, a London-based business, uses local farm-grown produce to make traditional preserves such as pear butter and quince cheese.

In 2000, a small wholesale market tucked under the railway arches at Borough, next to Southwark Cathedral, began holding a monthly specialist food market on Friday and Saturday mornings in an effort to regenerate the area. It rapidly became the haunt of food journalists, who in turn made it a popular destination for the public. Before long, Borough Market was open every week. Crowds thronged the market to soak up the atmosphere, enjoy roast chicken sandwiches, and buy wonderful specialist foods ranging from freshly roasted coffee to London honey. You can assemble a dinner party menu in minutes by pushing your way through the crowds to Turnips, where you can buy armfuls of tomatoes, basil, peaches, and fresh figs, or to Brindisa, where you can select saffron and rice for paella, or salt cod, olive oil, vinegars, and almonds. Chefs drop in to Borough Market to seek out new suppliers. Many of the stall holders, such as the Ginger Pig and L'Artisan du Chocolat, became so popular that they expanded into smart retail premises across London.

FLAVORS OF THE NEIGHBORHOODS

One of the best ways to explore London is to talk to the locals and quiz them about where and what they eat. Your search for food will lead you to discover the hidden side of London, from a cabbie's favorite fish-and-chip restaurant to a food lover's secret vice, a fabulous cookbook shop.

Despite its vast size, London is made up of many small neighborhoods. Each is a world within itself, housing countless different nationalities, cultures, and foods. Every district is filled with intriguing shops, restaurants, cafés, and bars. Some date back centuries; others are creating the latest trends.

The South Bank

A pedestrian walk that runs along the south side of the Thames, the South Bank links the Royal Festival Hall with the Hayward Gallery and Shakespeare's Globe Theatre. In recent years it has become a mecca for Londoners who like to brunch at Tate Modern and view the exhibits before strolling along to Borough Market to buy food for the weekend, such as coffee from Monmouth Coffee House, cheese from Neal's Yard Dairy, and cakes from Konditor & Cook. Many also walk eastward to enjoy the view of the Tower of London while eating simple modern British dishes such as beet salad with horseradish and poached egg or roast squab with balsamic vinegar, shallots, and sage at the Blueprint Café in the Design Museum. For some, there is nothing better than a play at the National Theatre or the Old Vic, followed by a takeaway of crisp-fried cod from Masters Super Fish on Waterloo Road.

The City and East End

At the heart of London lies the City, with its shimmering office blocks, medieval churches, and Roman ruins. This is the capital's financial center, yet its past endures in old markets such as Spitalfields, Leadenhall, and Smithfield. Tiny ancient pubs are tucked away in alleyways. Among its superb restaurants are Smiths of Smithfield and Club Gascon. The former serves hearty dishes of rare breed meats, such as grilled Longhorn rump steak, while the latter offers a constant flow of small plates, such as smoked zander (a white, freshwater fish) on a hot stone. Heading up Commercial Street, you'll find the utilitarian-looking St. John Bread & Wine, where the Whitechapel crowd of artists hangs out and enjoys simple British food from a bacon sarnie to rhubarb ice cream. A few more steps eastward takes you to Brick Lane, with its colorful Bengali shops such as the Taj stores and a branch of the Ambala Sweet Centre.

Soho

During the day Soho has a slightly scruffy, Bohemian feel, beloved of its residents, whom you can find sipping coffee in one of the many Italian bars, grabbing a spicy Caribbean bite at Mr. Jerk, or wandering down Berwick Street Market to buy some asparagus or early Jersey Royals (new potatoes) for supper. The area abounds with free-thinking media and celebrity types who hang out in private clubs such as the Groucho Club. Restaurants range from Soho institutions like L'Escargot and Pollo, the latter offering inexpensive Italian

fare, to relative newcomers, among them the elegant Lindsay House, serving superlative Irish food in pared-down eighteenth-century rooms. At night, Soho is transformed by the young pleasure seekers who throng its many restaurants, bars, pubs, and clubs. Favorites are Yauatcha, Milk & Honey, and Ronnie Scott's Jazz Club.

Chinatown

Chinatown is renowned for its bustling chaos and rude manner, both of which Londoners enjoy, regarding them as integral to the area's unique atmosphere. The narrow, old streets are filled with Chinese restaurants, gambling clubs, supermarkets, and other businesses, as well as tourists. During the day, boxes of durian fruit, water spinach, and other exotic produce spill out from crowded shops like Loon Fung Supermarket and S. W. Trading Ltd. Dim sum addicts queue up at restaurants such as Chuen Cheng Ku, Royal Dragon, or New World, especially on weekends, to feast on yam rolls, lobster dumplings, and sautéed

turnip paste. At night, the restaurants fill with diners eager to sample the steamed crab doused in Shaoxing wine at Mr. Kong, the famous wind-dried meat dishes at Poons, and the Shanghai cuisine served at Ecapital.

Knightsbridge

The well-heeled shoppers who frequent Knightsbridge like to dress up before they go out. They live in the hushed world of embassies, five-star hotels, and the fashion stores that stretch from Hyde Park to Sloane Square. Rather than venture into a super-market, they prefer to order a cold lobster and *fraises de bois* from the food halls of Harvey Nichols or Harrods, and choose from a glittering array of Michelin-starred restau-rants including Nahm, serving classic Thai food; Zafferano, with its stylish, modern Italian menu; and Foliage, Petrus, and the Capital Restaurant, which offer a distinctively London style of British-French cooking. With the exception of the discreet Zafferano, all are housed in hotels. The young set likes to hang

out at Zuma, known for its elegant Japanese food, and at Mr. Chow's, where superb Chinese food is presented in a glamorous setting.

Chelsea

This sprawling area that runs from Knights-bridge down to the Thames was once the haunt of artists and punk rockers. It is now dominated by wealthy thirty-somethings who spend their time buying wares in David Mellor's lovely kitchen shop. When shopping for food, they buy their groceries from the chic food shops of Elizabeth Street and pick up choco-lates from L'Artisan du Chocolat. Most impor-tant, some of London's finest restaurants are close by, including the eponomously named establishments of chefs Gordon Ramsay and Tom Aikens. London's best Indian restaurant, Rasoi Vineet Bhatia, is also in Chelsea.

Notting Hill

Notting Hillbillies, as they are known, are unlike other Londoners in their combination of flashiness and social conscience. The area

where they live stretches from Notting Hill to Ladbroke Grove and Westbourne Park Road Grove. This was one of the city's first neighborhoods to have organic shops such as Fresh & Wild and Planet Organic. Notting Hill is also home to Books for Cooks on Blenheim Crescent, laid-back gastropubs including the Cow and the Oak, and the stylish yet unpretentious Sardinian restaurant Assaggi, whose dining room is above a pub in Chepstow Villas. Those in search of local glitz tend to hang out at the pan-Asian fusion restaurant E&O, while those who prefer to be transported to a more unusual part of the world might go to Mandola, a tiny Sudanese restaurant.

Southall

Suburban Southall has been an Indian neighborhood since the 1950s. Every weekend, its main street, the Broadway, is transformed into a bustling Indian bazaar filled with the scent of spicy grilled kebabs and the blare of Bhangra music. The crowd jostles and pushes good-naturedly as people stop to bargain for a box of guavas or eye up the queue for Indian sweets in the Ambala Sweet Centre. Traditionally dressed women stock up on spices, pulses, and pickles at shops like Sira Cash & Carry before gazing into the jewelry shops. Late into the night, entire families treat themselves to *chaat* at the brightly lit Gifto's Lahore Karahi or a meal at popular Madhu's, where Kenyan Punjabi food is served.

Marylebone

Marylebonites are a social breed of Londoners who love the gentle pace of their eighteenth-century neighborhood with its stylish shops and weekly farmers' market. The area stretches south from Marylebone Road to Oxford Street and west from Great Portland Street to Edgware Road. Patisserie Valerie on Marylebone High Street and the many pubs, such as the Marylebone Tup or Dusk, are popular with neighborhood residents. The area is filled with restaurants, ranging from the casual, yet elegant No. 6 on George Street to the sophisticated Michelin-starred Orrery, which serves contemporary French food. Other neighborhood favorites include fish and chips at the Golden Hind and exceptional Italian food at Locanda Locatelli.

Mayfair

The grand sweep of Park Lane separates Mayfair from the green open spaces of Hyde Park. Bordered to the south by Green Park, to the north by Oxford Street, and to the east by Regent Street, Mayfair is home to some of London's grandest hotels, including the Ritz, the Dorchester, Claridges, the Connaught, and the Metropolitan, as well as some of London's well-known Michelin-starred restaurants. The Gavroche serves classic French food, while the Square offers superb modern British food. Londoners love straying into Mayfair's elegant streets, whether for brunch at Le Truc Vert after a walk in the park, for lunch at Nicole's after window-shopping in Bond Street, or for a teatime treat at Sketch. The neighborhood's tiny lanes contain hidden gems such as small pubs where locals can savor a pint of beer.

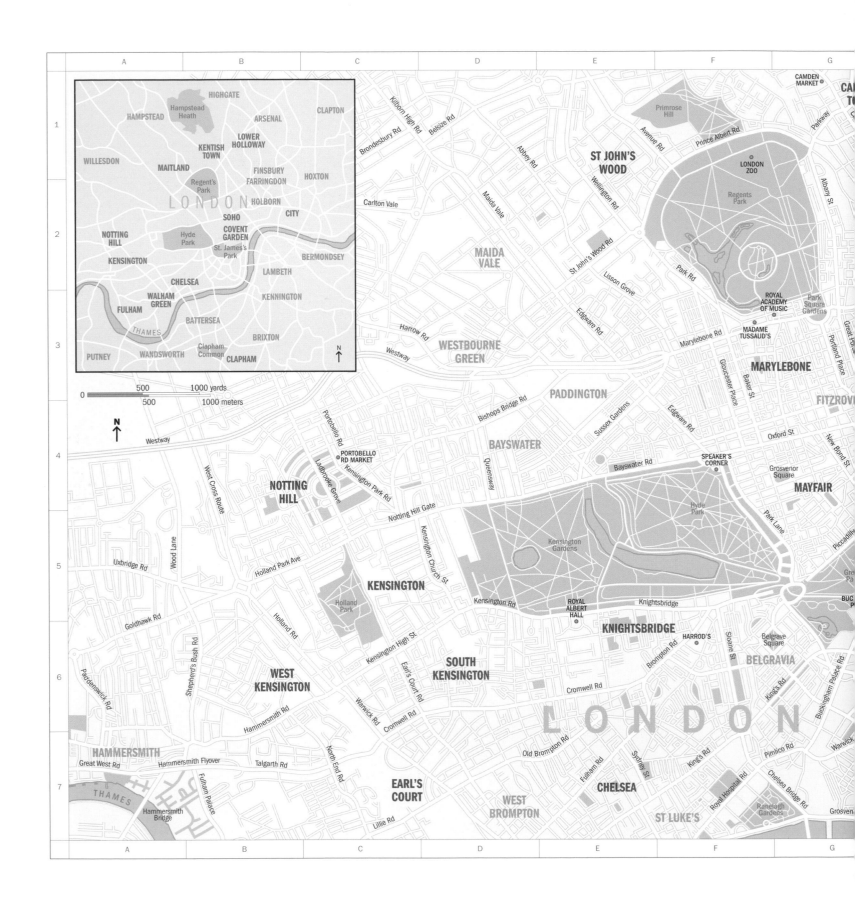

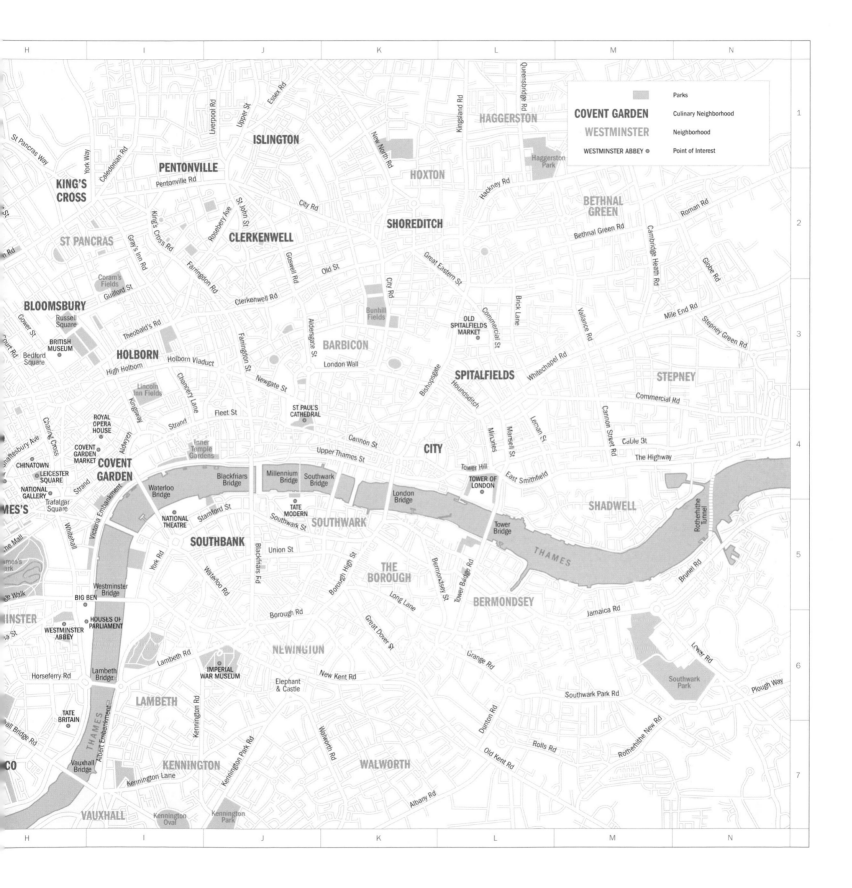

Best of **LONDON**

The thought of afternoon tea conjures rich images, from a lavish spread in the drawing room of a grand country house to the eccentricities of the Mad Hatter and his outsized teapot in *Alice's Adventures in Wonderland.* Regardless of where it is observed, teatime is a treat—without it, life would be much less pleasurable.

AFTERNOON TEA

In gentler times, the ceremony of afternoon tea had a certain grace. Women would dress in their best frocks and would sport both hats and gloves. The event served more than the mere social function of meeting and gossiping, however. It was an occasion at which people could be entertained informally, without the rigidity that often pervaded lunch or dinner.

It was de rigueur to offer a tiered cake stand of dainty sandwiches, scones, sponge cake, and fruit cake, alongside a plate of hot buttered English crumpets. Homemade jam and clotted cream—a Cornish and Devonshire specialty made by heating cream in a shallow enamel pan until it forms a honeycomb crust —were, and remain, staple accompaniments to the floury scone. Politeness dictated that you began with the savory items before moving on to the sweet.

The art of laying a table for tea was almost as important as the food itself. There would be a white lace tablecloth, lace-edged linen napkins, fine bone china, a highly polished silver tea service, and, perhaps, a mother-of-pearl jam spoon with which to delve into the cut-glass jam pot. Teacups would be rinsed out with hot water before pouring in the tea, to prevent the delicate china from cracking.

Afternoon tea was particularly fashionable during the Edwardian period between 1901 and 1910. When the Argentinian tango arrived in Britain in 1910, London's grand hotels began to host tea dances, to the accompaniment of a live orchestra. By the early 1920s, the tea dance had become so popular that it continued to be an important social event until World War II. The Savoy Hotel and the Waldorf Astoria still maintain the tradition

today, encouraged by the recent revival of interest in ballroom dancing.

In contrast to the high style of these hotels and that of their peers, the Connaught and the Ritz, many tea drinkers enjoy the rural romance of The Orangery in Kensington Gardens. Others prefer the sleek sophistication of Sketch on Conduit Street, whose tiny cakes can be savored with an exquisite cup of jasmine tea. The wit of the "Prêt-à-Portea" served in the Caramel Room at the fashionable Berkeley Hotel draws a stylish clientele. Each tiny sandwich or miniature cake is inspired by the latest fashion on the season's catwalks. For a more exotic approach, Londoners visit Yauatcha, on Broadwick Street, which offers delectable cakes in the French tradition but with an Asian twist, and an extraordinary range of Chinese teas.

The quintessentially British ritual is an indulgent respite during a busy day.

VICTORIA SPONGE

COCONUT RASPBERRY SLICES

FINGER SANDWICHES

LEMON MERINGUE PIE

HOT CROSS BUNS

VICTORIA SPONGE

Named after Queen Victoria, who liked to serve it at tea, this plain but delicious cake has the perfect balance of ingredients, achieved by matching the weight of the eggs in their shells with the same weight each of softened butter, sugar, and self-rising flour. The light batter is baked in two cake pans until golden. Once cooled, it is typically filled with raspberry jam and whipped cream or buttercream frosting, then dusted liberally with confectioners' (icing) sugar.

LEMON MERINGUE PIE

Londoners are partial to all kinds of lemon tarts. Lemon meringue pie (the term "pie" is occasionally used for tarts in Britain) is a favorite for tea or dessert. Crisp shortcrust pastry is filled with tangy lemon curd and topped with meringue. The original recipe is thought to date back to 1868.

COCONUT RASPBERRY SLICES

Biscuits are a daily essential, often eaten with a midmorning cup of coffee or as part of afternoon tea. Chewy variations, such as these shortbread slices with raspberry jam and coconut, are very popular.

FINGER SANDWICHES

Delicate and dainty, slender finger sandwiches, with their crusts removed, are the epitome of an elegant tea. Three fillings are traditional. Two are served on white bread: sliced cucumber, and chopped hard-boiled egg combined with mayonnaise and cress. Brown bread is preferred for wafer-thin slices of smoked salmon, with a squeeze of lemon juice and a fine grinding of pepper. Tea sandwiches should be prepared close to serving time to ensure freshness. The sandwiches are served on a paper or lace doily to absorb any moisture.

HOT CROSS BUNS

It is traditional to eat hot cross buns—split, toasted, and buttered—for breakfast on Good Friday. Currants, finely chopped candied citrus peel, cinnamon, and nutmeg are added to an enriched dough that is shaped into small balls, then adorned with a pastry cross (in commemoration of Christ's crucifixion) and baked. Originally, the dough balls were marked with a cross prior to baking to ward off evil spirits that might prevent them from rising, and on Good Friday, this practice is still observed. Once cooled, these specialties are glazed.

JOLLY RICH FRUITCAKE

COFFEE AND WALNUT CAKE

FONDANT FANCIES

SCONES

CRUMPETS

COFFEE AND WALNUT CAKE

Every café and cake shop in London offers a tempting array of cakes in all shapes and sizes. An enduring favorite is the coffee and walnut cake. Made from layers of moist walnut sponge sandwiched together by thick coffee butter or cream cheese icing, it is topped with the same luscious icing or occasionally with white fondant icing. Walnut halves or chopped walnuts are used for decoration. Every customer expects to be served a large slice, blissfully closing their eyes as they savor their first bite.

FONDANT FANCIES

For afternoon tea, many of the grand London hotels present a silver tier filled with tiny cakes, scones, and sandwiches. No tier is complete without a few fondant fancies: fondant-coated, square variations of a fairy cake.

CRUMPETS

A British favorite, crumpets are made from a thick, yeasted batter that is cooked on a griddle. The thick disk is perforated with tiny, spongy holes. Small packets of crumpets are sold in corner shops and supermarkets. They are served toasted with lots of butter.

JOLLY RICH FRUITCAKE

Londoners often bring a slice of moist fruitcake on a long walk or to picnics in the park. Fruitcake is like an energy bar, tightly packed with dark raisins, golden raisins (sultanas), and dried currants. It contains little sugar, flour, and eggs. The dried fruit is usually macerated in rum or brandy, before the remaining ingredients—candied peel, cinnamon, allspice, cloves, and nuts—are added. The baked cake can then be "fed" with a spirit or liqueur for an added kick. Northerners, particularly from Yorkshire and Lancashire, like eating fruitcake with Cheddar cheese.

SCONES

Originating in Scotland, the scone is a staple of British afternoon tea. The dough, enriched with butter and eggs, is gently mixed with buttermilk, sour milk, or cream. Scones were traditionally cooked on a griddle but nowadays are baked in an oven. They are split and liberally buttered while warm. Sweet scones contain a little sugar and sometimes golden raisins (sultanas) or currants, and are delicious with clotted cream and jam. The savory variety can include such embellishments as Cheddar cheese or fresh herbs.

Londoners were formally introduced to the charms of tea in 1664, when the East India Company began to import it from China. Coffeehouses soon sold tea for home consumption—a habit that Catherine of Braganza, wife of Charles II, encouraged through her own predilection for the beverage.

TEA MERCHANTS AND TEA

By 1707, when Fortnum & Mason began to sell tea, it was well established as a fashionable, if expensive, drink. While men enjoyed it in coffeehouses, gentlewomen made clear green or black tea in the Chinese style, without milk or sugar, for their guests in the evening. Then, in 1717, Thomas Twining opened a tea shop—known by the sign of the Golden Lyon—in Devereaux Court and established the tradition of respectable ladies going out for tea. Tea gardens such as those at Ranelagh and Vauxhall followed, where all and sundry drank tea, danced, and watched public entertainments.

Tea only became widely available to the poor in 1784 when the government removed the high excise duty on tea leaves. Midmorning tea breaks were routine by the end of the nineteenth century. At many firms,

a "tea lady" was employed to wheel a trolley around the office, which contained a vast urn of strong black tea, milk, sugar, and biscuits. The creation of afternoon tea, or simply "tea" as the British call it, is credited to Anna, seventh Duchess of Bedford, who, in the early 1800s, grew so hungry between lunch and dinner that she served tea with nibbles at four or five in the afternoon. "High tea" developed in the north of England during the nineteenth century, when working families merged tea and supper to create a single meal at six at which various cold meats, breads, and cakes were accompanied by tea.

Today, tea consumption has been revitalized with the availability of rare and unusual varieties from such companies as Twinings and Fortnum & Mason. Fortnum's, as it is affectionately known, has furnished

many a pantry with a caddy of one of its famous teas, of which there are some 140, including the popular Royal Blend—a combination of Ceylon and Assam—dating to the coronation of Edward VII in 1902. Twinings and Fortnum's have been trading tea for nearly three hundred years. Twinings's museum, at the back of its shop, is well worth visiting, and its Lady Grey tea—a sumptuous blend of Chinese leaves and orange and lemon peel, flavored with a hint of bergamot— is the perfect item to take home as a memento. Whittard, a relative newcomer since 1886, has done much to promote tea as a twenty-first-century beverage. It has many outlets, and those in fashionable Covent Garden and Carnaby Street have Tea Zones, stations where you can create customized blends by combining the leaf and flavor of your choice.

Confidences are often exchanged over a fragrant cup of tea.

Appreciated centuries ago for its reviving qualities, a cup of sweet, strong tea is still regarded by many Londoners as a cure-all for minor ailments and fatigue. It is as though the very act of putting on the kettle helps set the world right. Morning, noon, or night, the fragrance of brewing tea helps soothe the spirit and compose the mind.

The Bramah Museum of Tea and Coffee

Since tea is a national institution, it is not surprising that London is home to the world's first museum celebrating the drinking of it. The Bramah Museum of Tea and Coffee near London Bridge has a collection of historical tea-making ephemera and an adjoining tearoom. It sells everything you need for a perfect "cuppa": a range of specialist teas, teapots, cozies, strainers, pitchers for milk and hot water, sugar bowls, and tongs.

Understanding Tea

Tea is made from the leaves of two different evergreen bushes. One is *Camellia sinensis,* which originated in China. The slightly larger-leafed, more prolific *Camellia assamica* originated in Assam. There are three main categories, defined by how tea is processed: green (unfermented), black (fermented), and oolong (semifermented). For green tea, the leaves are dried immediately after picking to prevent oxidation and activation of the enzymes that change the taste of the tea. This ensures that the tea retains a fresh, almost grassy taste. In contrast, leaves for black tea are wilted to reduce moisture, bruised by rolling, and then allowed to brown further by contact with air so they oxidize. Oxidization gives black tea a full and complex taste. Oolong teas, made from large-leafed plants, are partially oxidized. The best are Formosa oolongs. White teas, predominantly from the downy tips of the unopened leaf bud, are dried naturally in the sun. Tea can also be classified by its country of origin and by the size of the tea leaves.

Making the Perfect Pot of Tea

BOILING THE WATER The water should be brought just to a boil for brewing black tea and be just off a boil, at 160°–190°F (70°–88°C), for preparing more delicate green or white teas. The ideal pot for brewing tea contains a small, perforated holder for the tea leaves. The holder can be removed or sealed with a plunger once the tea has been brewed sufficiently.

BREWING THE TEA LEAVES The teapot is warmed with hot water just before the leaves are added. Traditionally, British tea drinkers allow 1 teaspoon of loose-leaf tea per person, plus 1 extra teaspoon for the pot, but most tea experts recommend experimenting to taste. Large-leaf teas can be brewed for 4–5 minutes; small-leaf teas need only 2–3 minutes.

SERVING THE TEA Britons drink their tea black or white (with milk), or with a slice of lemon. There is much debate about the correct way to serve the milk, but most believe that to prevent the milk from tasting scalded, it should be poured into the cup before the tea is slowly added.

BREAKFAST

CHAMOMILE INFUSION

EARL GREY

JASMINE

BREAKFAST

If Britons feel strongly about one culinary subject, it is their breakfast beverage. Tea drinkers are appalled at the idea of drinking coffee in the morning, while coffee drinkers cannot abide tea. Most tea drinkers love the strong, full-bodied taste of a traditional English breakfast tea, a blend of black Assam and Ceylon teas, which they drink with milk. Some prefer the even stronger Irish breakfast tea, a blend of Assam and Kenyan teas that is renowned for its robust taste. Both are perfect for enhancing the delights of bacon, eggs, and toast with marmalade.

CHAMOMILE INFUSION

Londoners are very fond of herbal infusions, where a flower or herb is steeped in hot water to extract its flavor. They particularly like organic chamomile, which they drink late at night as a relaxant. Perforated sachets of the chamomile flowers are infused with barely boiled water for about 3 minutes to release the delicate, fresh flavor.

EARL GREY

The flowery scent of bergamot wafting on the afternoon air is sufficient to alert everyone that it is tea time. The aroma comes from Earl Grey, a British tea created in the eighteenth century reputedly in honor of the second Earl Grey. Traditionally, it is made by flavoring a blend of black Darjeeling and China teas with oil of bergamot, an intensely aromatic variety of orange. Some brands of Earl Grey include a touch of Lapsang Souchong, which imbues the tea with a smoky taste. Earl Grey is perfect for afternoon tea, preferably without lemon or milk.

JASMINE

Long a London favorite, jasmine was first sipped in Chinese restaurants. It is now sold throughout the city. Most jasmine tea is produced in China's Fujian province from green tea leaves that are picked in spring and then placed close by or layered with fresh jasmine flowers in summer. The process can be repeated up to seven times until the tea is perfumed with the blooms' intense fragrance. Sometimes the tea leaves are rolled into tiny pearls that unfurl in hot water. Jasmine tea is delicious with dim sum or elegant cakes.

MOROCCAN MINT   JAPANESE GREEN   DARJEELING    LAPSANG SOUCHONG

MOROCCAN MINT

This aromatic herbal infusion is offered on the menus of all chic London restaurants and is favored by fashion-conscious women who want a stylish, noncaffeinated drink. The best is found in Middle Eastern cafés, where fresh Moroccan mint leaves are infused in boiling water, then poured into tiny ornate cups and sweetened to taste with sugar.

JAPANESE GREEN

With the spread of Japanese restaurants in London, the taste for Japanese green teas has become a refreshing alternative to traditional British teas. Green teas are drunk at any time of the day. Many devotees seek out Japanese cups for savoring the exquisite flavor. The finest teas, Gyokura (Precious Dew), are grown under reed mats for 20 days in April to produce thick, soft, bright green leaves. After picking, the leaves are steamed, rolled, and dried to preserve their fresh taste. They need to be infused for only 2 minutes in hot, not boiling, water.

DARJEELING

The delicate flavor of Darjeeling tea makes it one of the most highly regarded black teas in Britain. It is favored for afternoon tea with a slice of lemon or milk, but is drunk anytime. Grown high in the foothills of the Himalayas, Darjeeling has a light astringency. Many tea aficionados prefer the second flush for its slightly heavy, muscatel-like flavor. Specialty grocers such as Fortnum & Mason offer an amazing array of single-estate Darjeelings, including the floral-tasting first-flush Margaret's Hope and the unusual white Darjeeling from Castleton.

LAPSANG SOUCHONG

Londoners like tea with character, and Lapsang Souchong clearly falls into this category. This black China tea blend is easily recognizable by its tarry aroma and smoky taste. It is always served black or with lemon, usually in the afternoon and preferably with tiny smoked salmon sandwiches followed by a slice of walnut cake. The unique taste of Lapsang Souchong is partly the result of smoking the tea leaves after they have been dried. This characteristic makes the tea especially refreshing on a sultry summer day.

Since Roman times, Londoners have enjoyed the finest foods from around the world. Over the centuries, the city's great port on the Thames has been the destination of ships laden with delicacies, from Italian olives and New World chiles to Indian cardamom and West Indian pineapples.

DELICATESSENS

Walking across London, you can get a feel for the city's recent history by the type of delicatessen you find. Soho, for example, still has a few wonderful old-fashioned Italian delis, such as Camisa & Son (founded in 1929) on Old Compton Street and Lina Stores (1930) on Brewer Street, which marked the influx of Italian immigrants early in the twentieth century. As you stroll past the doors, you are tempted by the scent of salamis and Parmesan cheese, and once inside, you cannot resist buying fresh pumpkin ravioli or dipping into a sack of dried green flageolet beans. When in Bayswater, you will notice the small delicatessens that cater to the Greeks who have been coming to worship at the Greek Orthodox cathedral of Aghia Sophia for well over a century. The Athenian Grocery on Moscow Road, like its neighboring shops, brims in the

summer with fresh grapevine leaves, green almonds, and sugar-dusted Turkish delight.

Wander through Marylebone, and you will find smart delicatessens that reflect the tastes of the area's well-heeled residents. At Speck on Marylebone High Street, you will be offered a morsel of aged pecorino or marinated artichoke hearts wrapped in prosciutto to sample before you have even perused the fresh pasta, peppery olive oil, and marinated anchovy fillets. When you enter La Fromagerie on Moxon Street, you will want to linger over the incredible array of European cheeses before looking at the specialty foods such as French violet liqueur, Italian roast coffee beans, fresh Amalfi lemons, and Sri Lankan peppercorns. On the other side of Marylebone, on Great Portland Street, lies Villandry, with its astounding range of foods, such as luscious

Danish pastries, English bacon, chutneys, myriad sea salts, and piccalilli—a spicy mustard and vegetable pickle. Unlike older delis in London, these shops have tables where you can sip coffee or tea or dine on the specially made dishes, which you can also take home.

In the past, specialty grocers traditionally catered to the wealthy. In Roman times, London gourmands paid high prices for liquamen (fermented fish sauce), pine nuts, raisins, and olive oil imported from the Mediterranean. By the fifteenth century, canny medieval merchants were making their fortunes by importing costly sugar and expensive spices such as peppercorns, saffron, ginger, and cloves. As overseas trade grew, prices slowly dropped, and new imports were added to the array of edible delights.

Visiting a local deli will reveal more about a neighborhood than any guidebook.

The Elizabethans, for example, were offered fresh oranges, candied citrus, and Parmesan cheese alongside spices, sugar, and dried fruits. By the eighteenth century, London was filled with specialist grocers and what were known as Italian warehouses. The latter were often started by Italian importers of olive oil, but they soon branched out to include such goods as rice, salt-preserved anchovies, dried macaroni, olives, and powdered cocoa, as well as exotic ingredients like soy, tamarind, and spicy sauces. Some merchants, such

foie gras terrine, pig's cheek in Armagnac, and freshly baked Gascony breads and pies.

It is easy to lose a sense of London's vast size, and even its inhabitants regard the city as a collection of densely populated villages, each with its own character. Some areas, such as Chiswick, have well-established delis that understand the preferences of local residents and cater to them accordingly. Mortimer & Bennett on Turnham Green Terrace supplies Chiswickites with specialty foods, mainly French and Italian, such as fine

Walking across London, you can get a feel for the city's recent history and diversity by the type of delicatessens that you find.

as Fortnum & Mason, began making potted beef, game in aspic, and other foods for customers to take home.

By the nineteenth century, the practice of purchasing prepared foods developed into another British institution: the hamper. On great social occasions such as Derby Day, members of London society would queue outside Fortnum & Mason in their carriages to collect picnic hampers of lobster salad and veal pies before driving down to the races at Epsom Downs. Hampers are now supplied by many delicatessens, including the other two grand food halls, Selfridges and Harrods.

Having retained the eclectic taste of their predecessors, Londoners consider it natural to use ingredients from around the world in their cooking. Most tend to patronize the shops nearest their work and home. Edgware Road locals, for instance, meander along the food aisles at the Lebanese delicatessen Green Valley on Upper Berkeley Street, considering what they might make with fruity-sour pomegranate syrup or dried fava (broad) beans. Shoppers passing through Smithfield stop off at the airy Comptoir Gascon on Charterhouse Street. Linked to the Michelin-starred Club Gascon, the shop sells its own

French conserves and fruit syrups, pâtés, and more than thirty different oils. In areas that have been without delis, the opening of one often heralds social change. The arrival of Brindisa in Exmouth Market was a sign that Clerkenwell, with its converted loft spaces and bars, was becoming fashionable. The specialty at Brindisa is Spanish food, from salt cod and Iberico hams to superlative almonds, paprika, and saffron, and the deli now supplies many London restaurants and other shops.

Only one London delicatessen is dedicated to British food: A. Gold on Brushfield Street near Liverpool Street Station. Situated in the smallest imaginable space, the shop is part of an eighteenth-century terrace and looks like an establishment out of the pages of a Charles Dickens novel. Here, you can find delicious King's English pork pies, potted shrimp from Morecambe Bay, English apple juices, quince liqueur, local beer brewed in Hoxton, and London rooftop honey. Beekeeping has become a popular hobby among Londoners, who keep hives in tiny rooftop gardens. Some of the honey is collected and sold by the London Honey Company. Shoppers rarely leave A. Gold without purchasing British sweets, whether toffee fudge or pink sugar mice.

British cheese making is enjoying an extraordinary renaissance, and London is the best place to sample some of the country's finest cheeses. Restaurants and shops offer a wonderful array of artisanal cheeses, from traditional favorites like creamy, savory Stilton to the newest farmhouse varieties.

CHEESEMONGERS AND CHEESE

Life without cheese is inconceivable to most Londoners. For centuries, regional British cheeses were sold in London alongside such imports as Italian Parmesan. Some regions, such as the Midlands, Cheshire, and Somerset became famous for their superb cow's milk cheese, namely Stilton, a blue cheese from the Midlands; Cheshire cheese, a white, salty, hard cheese; and Cheddar, a tangy hard cheese from Somerset.

In the middle of the last century, however, the making of artisanal cheese fell into decline as government policies encouraged the mass production of inexpensive food and many superb farmhouse cheeses did not conform to supermarket demands for packaged, easy-to-slice cheese. While Londoners consoled themselves by buying French and Italian cheeses instead, occasionally, at Christmas

for example, they would seek out Cheddar or Stilton from a traditional cheesemonger, such as Paxton and Whitfield, which has sold cheese from its shop on Jermyn Street since 1797.

The situation changed dramatically in the early 1980s, when Randolph Hodgson, a maker of *fromage frais* and yogurt, began to sell wonderful, but virtually unknown, British and Irish cheeses from his Neal's Yard Dairy in Covent Garden. Customers squeezed into the tiny shop overflowing with fragrant drums of Devonshire Beenleigh Blue, truckles of mature Appleby's Cheshire, and creamy rounds of Milleens from County Cork. The cheeses vanished as customers tasted the difference between farmhouse specialties and the mass-produced products sold in supermarkets. Soon Hodgson was driving around the country in search of artisanal

cheese makers. Knowing that they had an outlet for their products, cheese makers began to develop new varieties, such as Spenwood, a hard, mild sheep's milk cheese from Berkshire. Others produced new versions of continental cheeses, such as Cerney, an ash-coated fresh goat cheese from Gloucestershire. Cheese-mongers and delis across the capital began selling regional cheeses again.

Another influence on Londoners' taste in cheese was La Fromagerie, opened by Patricia Michelson in Highbury in 1991. In 1995, with the aid of Eric Demelle, she began to perfect the French art of *affinage,* the process of maturing cheeses to further develop their taste and texture. The cheeses of La Fromagerie develop an intense, fruity taste and unctuous texture through *affinage.* Both Neal's Yard Dairy and La Fromagerie have opened second shops.

Ploughman's is a perfect pub lunch—fine cheese, fresh bread, and tangy pickle.

La Fromagerie

2-4 Moxon Street W1
Tel/Fax 020 7935 0341

OPEN EVERY DAY

Specialist Cheese Shop with
Wines, Selected Produce
& Café

Open all day serving
breakfast, lunch and
afternoon tea

Enjoy classic brunch fare
at weekends or a
la Fromagerie Picnic
in the park

STILTON

WIGMORE

DORSTONE

BERKSWELL

STILTON

Traditionally eaten at the end of a meal, and in greatest demand over Christmas, Stilton has an intense, savory taste and a creamy texture. Every Stilton-producing dairy follows its own recipe. Colston Bassett is still made in the traditional way in Nottinghamshire by ladling, rather than pouring, the cow's milk curds into a mold, which gives the cheese a particularly creamy texture. After the Stilton has matured a little, it is pierced with needles to allow air into it and encourage the growth of blue veins.

WIGMORE

Britons love the understated, whether it is a wisp of a Philip Treacy–designed hat or a subtly fragrant, semisoft Wigmore cheese. The cheese is the creation of Anne Wigmore, an analytical cheese maker based in Berkshire, who set about creating new styles of cheese in the mid-1980s, including Waterloo and Spenwood. Wigmore is made from unpasteurized sheep's milk. To develop delicate flavor nuances, the curds are washed with water to dilute their acidic whey, then are left to ripen for up to six weeks, when the cheese acquires a bloomy rind.

DORSTONE

This lemony, soft, ash-coated goat cheese is made by Charlie Westhead at Neal's Yard Creamery in Dorstone. With its delicate, fresh taste and crumbly, velvety texture, Dorstone is typical of the type of cheese Londoners like to eat during the summer months. Matured for only about ten days, this fresh cheese has a subtle acidity and flavor that needs no accompaniment other than some crusty bread or crisp radishes. It is perfect for impromptu picnics or lazy summer lunches.

BERKSWELL

It has become fashionable in London to offer a single cheese at the end of a meal with oat cakes and perhaps quince cheese. One of the best varieties for serving in this style is Berkswell, a West Midlands cheese with a floral taste and fudgy texture, created in 1989 by the Fletcher family. The Fletchers transform the unpasteurized milk from their East Friesland sheep into a new interpretation of a Caerphilly, usually made from lightly pressed and brine-soaked cow's milk curds. Berkswell is matured in basket-weave molds, which imprint the exterior.

MRS. KIRKHAM'S LANCASHIRE

STINKING BISHOP

BEENLEIGH BLUE

CHEDDAR

MRS. KIRKHAM'S LANCASHIRE

For many years, traditionally made Lancashire was rarely seen outside the county; its crumbly texture and milky acidity were considered an acquired taste. In 1995, Randolph Hodgson, a London cheese seller, secretly entered Mrs. Kirkham's Lancashire cheese in the British Cheese Awards. It won Supreme Champion and became fashionable overnight. Mrs. Kirkham, like her mother and grandmother before her, meticulously mixed the cow's milk curds over three days, then molded and pressed them to make a golden, hard cheese wrapped in cheesecloth (muslin).

STINKING BISHOP

Londoners are prone to daydreaming about rural life, particularly when eating Charles Martell's pungent semisoft Gloucestershire cheese. Some of the milk for the cheese comes from Martell's small herd of rare-breed Gloucester cows. The rind is washed with perry (pear cider), made from a rare local variety of pear called Stinking Bishop. The cheese develops a pale orange rind and a soft, creamy center. The idea of saving an endangered cattle breed and a rare pear variety by making a delicious cheese makes Stinking Bishop appealing to Londoners.

BEENLEIGH BLUE

One of the first new British blue cheeses to arrive on the London restaurant scene in the 1980s, Beenleigh Blue is made from the milk of Dorset cross Friesland sheep by Sarie Cooper and Robin Congdon, founders of Ticklemore Cheese in Devon. Its sweet, nutty taste captivated London cheese eaters, who serve it with flowery dessert wine or crumble it into a watercress, pear, and walnut salad. Later, Ticklemore Cheese created a creamy, rich cow's milk blue cheese called Devon Blue and an intense-tasting goat's milk blue called Harbourne Blue.

CHEDDAR

Cheddar forms one of the ancient cornerstones of British cheese making. The name refers to a method of making cheese that originated around the Cheddar gorge in Somerset but spread throughout the county. By the seventeenth century, local farmers were pooling their cow's milk to make vast truckles of Cheddar that could be matured for a couple of years. The best modern clothbound Cheddars vary, from the creamy Lincolnshire Poacher, which has a sweet buttery taste, to the crumbly, tangy Montgomery's Cheddar from Somerset.

On a warm summer evening, many a London street is filled with the murmuring of voices and the clinking of glasses. These are the sounds of the pub, an institution so integral to London life that few could imagine the city without it.

PUBS

The pub, as licensed public houses are affectionately known, is there for everyone. It is a place to meet up for a quick drink after work, to enjoy an informal meal, or to linger quietly over a pint of beer. There are no rules about what you can drink. A gin and tonic, a nonalcoholic ginger beer, or a glass of wine is served as often as a pint of beer. The best pubs are warm and welcoming, providing a unique sense of egalitarianism savored over a pint of cool, aromatic bitters. The British do not, as is so often inferred, drink warm beer. Instead, they drink it at the natural cellar temperature of about 50°–55°F (10°–13°C), which allows the beer to continue maturing in its cask. As a result, it has a full flavor and a restrained natural carbonation.

London has around 5,500 pubs that vary greatly in style from a homely mews pub with

its cozy bar and quiet clientele to a hip-and-happening gastropub where diners share their tables with strangers as they tuck into a hearty crab salad or a seasonal apple crumble. Gastropubs, a relatively recent phenomenon, began in 1991, when the Eagle opened on Farringdon Road. Most are started by young chefs who take over neglected pubs in the hopes of making their name—an endeavor that is far easier than investing in an expensive city restaurant. The menu, chalked up on a blackboard, tends to consist of simply made food using fresh, high-quality, seasonal ingredients, for example, roast beet and fresh goat cheese salad or salmon with fennel, sorrel, and cucumber. A good wine list is usually offered along with the normal pub drinks. Gastropubs, such as the Coach & Horses on Ray Street and the Oak on

Westbourne Park Road, are proving very popular with Londoners who crave relaxed neighborhood restaurants.

Although the British often worry that their pub culture is in decline, the reality is that modern pubs are following a long tradition of adapting to the needs of the day. Fifteenth-century London was filled with coaching inns, taverns, and ale houses. Each served a different purpose. Taverns, for example, were visited for their fine French wines and port. The latter was drunk in vast quantities whenever the wine trade was interrupted by war with France. One of the most famous taverns was Pontack's on Abchurch Lane, which served Chateau Haut-Brion clarets to customers including Sir Christopher Wren and Jonathan Swift. The tavern's modern descendant is the wine bar.

The flavor of a good beer, like wine, develops as it is sipped.

Coaching inns resembled hotels. Lying along the highways of Britain, they offered accommodation, food, drink, and stabling, as well as a good source of news from the mail coaches. Only one has survived in London—the George Inn on Borough High Street in Southwark, established in the 1540s during the reign of Henry VIII. Here, you can linger over a fruity, dry Greene King Abbot Ale (from Suffolk), in much the same way one of the inn's earlier patrons, William Shakespeare, might have done with earlier brews. Southwark was a wild place in the

which by the beginning of the eighteenth century was sold to Londoners as Guinness.

Today, barely a handful of London breweries remain: Fuller, Smith & Turner (founded in 1845) in Chiswick, and Young & Co.'s Brewery in Wandsworth (1831) are the oldest; Pitfield Brewery (1980) in Hoxton and Meantime Brewing (2000) in Greenwich are the youngest. Many traditional London beers are "bitters," an English term for a well-hopped ale imbued with a deep bitterness and a mild acidity. A mild ale is lightly hopped but has a full-bodied flavor.

London has around 5,500 pubs that vary greatly in style from classic, cozy bars to hip gastropubs where the food is the focus.

playwright's day. Situated beyond the reach of the city's ordinances, it was consequently awash with theaters, brothels, and bear rings. Coaching inns went into decline with the arrival of railways in the nineteenth century.

Ale houses are widely regarded as the direct ancestor of the public house. As their name implies, they served ale, a brew made from fermented grain. In the early fifteenth century, hops were added to this brew to help preserve it. From that time, ale (unhopped) became beer (hopped). Technically, the word *beer* refers to all drinks that have been fermented with grain and seasoned with hops. The English, however, rarely apply this term to lager, porter, or stout.

Londoners have always drunk beers from all over England, including their own London brews. The latter were made with dark, malted barley, particularly from East Anglia, and aromatic Kentish, Herefordshire, and Worcestershire hops such Goldings or Fuggles. London Porter, a black, heavily hopped, and highly alcoholic beer, was created in London in the 1720s. It was exported to Ireland, where Arthur Guinness, a local brewer, produced his own version,

Different pubs offer different selections of beers. The choices are influenced by the brewery that owns the pub (independently owned pubs are known as freehouses). The Guinea, a small mews pub on Bruton Place in Mayfair, for instance, belongs to the Young's estate and is a good place to imbibe cask-conditioned, dry Young's Bitter or Young's Special. The Churchill Arms on Kensington Church Street is an example of a Fuller's pub. Customers can choose from an array of Fuller's beers including the flowery Chiswick Bitter, the more complex London Pride, or the deeper-flavored Extra Special Bitter.

In contrast, the Greenwich Union is a modern pub on Royal Hill tied to Meantime Brewing, the brainchild of brew-master Alastair Hook. All the beers served at the pub come from his small brewery. Many are made in classic world styles, such as the delicate, fruity Cologne-style Kolsch and the light Bavarian wheat beer. Customers can request taster sets if they wish to sample a few beers before deciding on what to drink. Among the choices are the brewery's seasonals, including a light strawberry beer in summer and a chocolate stout in winter.

Just as the British have gained a renewed interest in native fish, it seems a cruel quirk of fate that the stocks from the ocean's larder have dwindled alarmingly from overfishing. This means that Londoners have to be far more selective about the fish they buy and where they buy it, resulting in an unprecedented and welcome focus on the provenance of seafood.

FISHMONGERS AND SEAFOOD

Fresh fish has long been an essential part of London life in both home kitchens and restaurants. In the eighteenth and nineteenth centuries, residents from all corners of society would sail down the river Thames to taverns in Greenwich and Dagenham for whitebait banquets. Before the arrival of the railways in 1838, most of London's fish came from nearby Barking, home to the world's largest commercial fishing fleet. In the winter months, ice was harvested from the surrounding lowlands, now part of London, to preserve the summer catch.

At one time, every London district had its own fishmonger, along with its own butcher, baker, and greengrocer. Today, fishmongers are an endangered species, as most people buy their seafood from supermarkets. Those businesses that survive owe their success to sustained local custom and a reputation for

carrying superb seafood. Some, such as the traditional and popular Golborne Fisheries in North Kensington, sell an enormous range of tropical fish, as well as indigenous fish and shellfish. Mauritian owner George Ng bypasses the Billingsgate Fish Market and sources his supply directly from overseas or from the Plymouth ports. Others, such as the Fish Shop on Kensington Church Street, are small but smart new enterprises that bring in fresh fare daily from the Cornish coast.

Steve Hatt, an Islington institution, and Walter Purkis & Sons on Muswell Hill are renowned fishmongers who sell a wide array of fine fish, from wild sea bass and prawns to home-smoked mackerel and haddock. More centrally located, on Paddington Street, is Blagden's, established in 1890 in a purpose-built fishmonger's, where shoppers always

find a seasonally changing display of British fish. Artfully arranged on the long marble slab might be Manx kippers one day and Scottish salmon the next.

Around the corner from Blagden's, on Marylebone High Street, is the newest branch of FishWorks (the other London location is the award-winning outlet in Chiswick), a clever concept that combines a fishmonger's counter with an adjoining seafood restaurant. A recent addition to the London scene, FishWorks sells and serves impeccable fish, offering simple but rarely seen dishes such as fried herring melts (roe) on toast. Chef and food writer Mitchell Tonks, the enterprising owner, sources his fish direct from the morning's landings at Newquay, Padstow, Fowey, and St. Mawes in Cornwall. FishWorks also has an efficient home-delivery service.

London fishmongers are blessed with access to some of the world's best seafood.

ENGLISH BROWN SHRIMP

EELS

EUROPEAN LOBSTER

COD

EELS

Inspiring appreciation and admiration, this serpentine fish makes its tenacious voyage from the Sargasso Sea to London's rivers and estuaries before it is caught on its homeward journey to spawn. The silvery adult eel is sold live and is prized for its delicate but richly flavored flesh. The East End's family-run pie-and-mash shops have been preparing it two ways for more than a century: cold and jellied with malt vinegar and bread and butter, and hot and stewed with liquor, a vivid green parsley sauce. It is also excellent smoked, served with horseradish.

ENGLISH BROWN SHRIMP

Shrimp have a fond place in the hearts of the British, their childhood summer holidays having been spent paddling in sand pools in an attempt to net them. Not to be confused with the American shellfish of the same name—known in London as prawns—these tiny delicacies are gray when alive, but take on a pinkish brown hue when briefly boiled. Traditionally served "potted" in butter spiced with mace, nutmeg, and cayenne, they are sublime with crusty bread. Shrimp can be added to creamy sauces, enveloped in mayonnaise, or turned into a shrimp bisque.

EUROPEAN LOBSTER

A quintessential ingredient of the British "season"—Wimbledon lawn-tennis championships, the Ascot races, and opera alfresco at Glyndebourne—the king of crustacea is caught between April and October and sold live. Its dark blue carapace and claws, which turn scarlet when cooked, yield dense, sweet white flesh, along with creamy meat from the head. The liver is used to enrich sauces, and the precious coral (eggs) to make a savory butter. The lobster is served cold, with herbed mayonnaise or lemon, or hot, drizzled with melted butter or a sophisticated sauce.

COD

Cod was once so prolific in North Atlantic waters that a thriving fishing port was located on the Thames estuary. Stocks have declined dramatically in recent years, and cod is becoming a scarce and expensive fish. As green or gray as the sea, with dappled lighter spots, this sleek creature has pearly white flesh that separates into firm, moist flakes, making it suitable for poaching, roasting, marinating, salting, and drying, and perfect in a fish pie. Deep-fried in golden batter, cod forms half of Londoners' favorite takeaway: fish and chips.

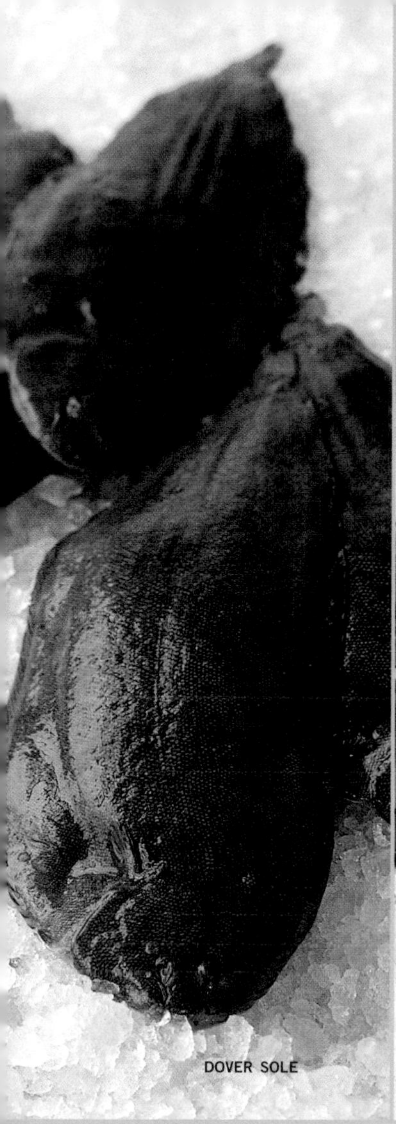

DOVER SOLE

BROWN CRAB

MACKEREL

WHITSTABLE OYSTERS

DOVER SOLE

Formerly a mainstay of classic English fish cookery, the exquisitely flavored Dover sole, which thrives in the cold waters of the North Sea, has become an expensive luxury. A small flatfish with both eyes on one side of its head, it is half sepia and half cream, with dark patches. The fine flavor of its firm but delicate flesh is best eaten simply: grilled with a savory butter, or accompanied by a delicate hollandaise sauce or beurre blanc. Sole is superb cooked on the bone or, once filleted, panfried, poached, or steamed.

BROWN CRAB

One of the finest crustaceans found in British waters, the brown crab is abundant and surprisingly inexpensive. The best specimens are caught far off shore, although traditional pots are still used in shallow waters. Often sold boiled, the crab is best presented as simply as possible: cold, with mayonnaise, lemon, and brown bread and butter. Fishmongers often sell prepared crab, separating white claw meat from brown body meat and mixing the latter with English mustard, chopped hard-boiled egg, and mayonnaise before piling the mixture back in the shell.

MACKEREL

This handsome fish has a svelte body cloaked in brilliant colors— shimmering metallic green-blue on top and silvery white on the underbelly. This oily fish spoils quickly and so is best eaten soon after being caught. The smaller specimens are best grilled or barbecued, while the larger are best stuffed and baked. All sizes benefit from being served with a piquant sauce or accompaniment to offset their richness. Gooseberry sauce is a classic choice, as is mustard butter. Mackerel is also delicious hot or cold smoked.

WHITSTABLE OYSTERS

In marked contrast to their current elevated status, these saltwater mollusks were once so prolific in Britain that they were bought by the barrel load and made into stews, soups, and fritters. Famed since Dickens's time, the south-coast Whitstable oyster is opened just before eating with a special knife and consumed live to savor the briny juice and capture the elusive flavor. The raw oysters are sometimes dressed with shallot vinegar or lemon. When cooked— bathed in cream, sprinkled with Parmesan cheese, dotted with butter, and grilled—they are divine.

As dusk falls over London, the pace of life quickens in readiness for the evening ahead. Bartenders are busy replenishing their bars with fresh fruit, herbs, and ice. Then they turn the lights low. The stage is set. It's time to party.

BARS AND COCKTAILS

Stylish new bars open all the time, keen to attract Londoners who enjoy experimenting with new cocktails. Experimentation and rivalry are rife among bartenders, which, along with the tolerant London lifestyle, attract other bartenders from around the world. They, in turn, introduce new ingredients and fresh ideas, which further fuels the vibrant cocktail scene.

Until the early 1990s, the London bar scene was, to put it kindly, old-fashioned. If you wanted a classic cocktail, you went to a hotel bar such as the Cocktail Bar at Duke's Hotel on St. James's Place or the Library Bar at the Lanesborough Hotel on Hyde Park Corner. The latter became famous under the auspices of Salvatore Calabrese, who created various drinks, including the breakfast martini, made with lime marmalade, Cointreau, lemon juice, and plenty of gin.

By 1994, thirty-something Londoners were tiring of their nightclub culture. They wanted more relaxed environments that featured late-night music. At the same time, Dick Bradsell, London's supreme mixologist, was becoming well known for his superb cocktails. When Oliver Peyton opened the glamorous Atlantic Bar & Grill in 1996, he employed Bradsell to design the cocktail list and named one of the bars after him. Bradsell's influence was felt throughout the London cocktail scene as he created drink menus for new bars. Many of London's best bartenders studied under him and tried to emulate his approach by sourcing the best and freshest ingredients for cocktails.

Within three years, the bar scene had taken off, with fashionistas drinking shots of fresh pineapple or watermelon vodka martinis at the minimalist Met Bar in the Metropolitan

Hotel and media types sipping Dick Bradsell's Match Spring Punch at Jonathan Downey's Match EC1 in Clerkenwell.

Gradually, a London cocktail ethos is developing. The use of bottled juices and mixers is frowned upon, and the best bars, such as the Townhouse on Beauchamp Place, Milk & Honey on Poland Street, and Floridita on Wardour Street, prepare their own juices and syrups, whether lime, pineapple, or ginger. Bartenders go to great lengths to source superlative spirits like Bramley & Gage quince liqueur or Havana Club three-year-old Cuban rum. Both classic and contemporary cocktail recipes are subjected to rigorous competition, and new cocktails are constantly evolving. Most important, London bartenders try to ensure that their customers' palates remain stimulated as the night drifts on.

Friends, music, and cocktails keep Londoners out until the early-morning hours.

PIMM'S

OLD-FASHIONED

MOJITO

MATCH SPRING PUNCH

THE BRAMBLE

PIMM'S

In the 1840s, James Pimm created a bitter gin sling for his London restaurant. It proved so popular that he bottled it commercially as Pimm's Cup No. 1 in 1859. Londoners tend to drink it during the summer, preferably by the river or at garden parties. The bitter gin Pimm's mixture is poured into a pitcher, then is diluted with lemonade and ice and flavored with lemon, borage flowers, and cucumber peel. Traditionally, the drink is served in a pint glass.

OLD-FASHIONED

Bourbon is enjoying a revival thanks to the classicist school of cocktails advocating beautifully made, traditional recipes. An orange slice, a maraschino cherry, bitters, and sugar are mixed in an old-fashioned glass, then bourbon, ice, and soda water are added.

MOJITO

Londoners love Cuba for its music, bars, and cigars. Consequently, London bartenders make lots of mojitos. They shake Havana rum with ice, bitters, soda water, fresh lime juice, mint, and sugar syrup before straining it over cracked ice.

THE BRAMBLE

English taste has been captured by this contemporary classic from renowned mixologist Dick Bradsell. The Bramble has an unusual musky flavor that comes from its *crème de mure,* blackberry liqueur. It is made by shaking two parts dry Tanqueray No. Ten gin, one part lemon juice, and a splash of sugar syrup with ice, then straining the mixture into a tumbler of crushed ice. After the drink is stirred, *crème de mure* is drizzled over the ice so that the deep purple liqueur swirls inklike into the liquid. The Bramble has become part of every London bartender's repertoire.

MATCH SPRING PUNCH

Concoct a long, bubbly, pink drink, and London women will love it, especially if accompanied by a plate of salty chips. This drink goes by two names. The Match Bars claim it as their own, as it was originally put on the first Match Bar menu in Clerkenwell by its creator, Dick Bradsell. Other bars call it Russian Spring Punch, Bradsell's original name for the drink. Vodka, lemon juice, sugar syrup, crème de cassis, raspberry liqueur, raspberries, and ice are shaken and strained into a tall glass with ice, then topped off with Champagne.

FLAVORED COLLINS

CHAMPAGNE COCKTAIL

VODKA ESPRESSO

CAIPIRINHA

NEGRONI

FLAVORED COLLINS

Two schools drive London cocktail fashion, the classicists and the experimentalists. The latter are influenced by Britain's top chefs. Flavored collinses, made by experimentalists, are typical of British taste—combining superb gin with a seasonal ingredient such as elderflower or blackberry. The gooseberry-flavored collins was created by London mixologist Nick Strangeway. Hendricks gin, gooseberry purée, fresh lemon juice, and lemon thyme syrup are mixed in a collins glass, then topped with soda water and garnished with lemon and a sprig of lemon thyme.

CHAMPAGNE COCKTAIL

At certain times of year, especially during Christmas and New Year's, Londoners like to pull out all the stops at home and offer guests Champagne cocktails and smoked salmon canapés. The Bellini, a combination of fresh peach purée, peach liqueur, and *prosecco,* may be more popular in summer, but it lacks the Champagne cocktail's sophisticated and subtle bitterness, a flavor that comes from a few drops of Angostura bitters soaked into a single sugar cube. A splash of good Cognac, such as Remy Martin, is added to the flute, followed by dry Champagne.

VODKA ESPRESSO

Londoners have a taste for coffee and alcohol. Combine them in a cocktail, and you have a classic London wake up drink. This is exactly what Dick Bradsell did in the 1990s when he devised his ice-cold vodka espresso, otherwise known as the Pharmaceutical Stimulant, for the über-hip bar at the now defunct Pharmacy in Notting Hill, which was co-owned and designed by British artist Damien Hirst. Vodka espresso is often made with Illy espresso and Finlandia vodka, plus a touch of Kahlúa, then is shaken with ice and strained into a glass.

CAIPIRINHA

Based on *cachaca,* a Brazilian spirit made from fresh sugarcane, the caipirinha is a delicious cocktail that takes time to mix properly. Tempered with muddled lime, brown sugar, and ice, the freshtasting result is worth the wait.

NEGRONI

London bartenders like nothing better than to sip a bittersweet Florentine Negroni after hours and mull over the evening's events. Made with vermouth, Campari, and Tanqueray gin, it is served in a cold old-fashioned glass, garnished with flamed orange peel.

Word spreads fast when a good artisanal bakery opens in London. Locals, as well as customers from farther afield, soon show up at the door, eager to try the tempting new selection of pastries and breads. Their biggest challenge is deciding what to order.

BAKERIES

London is such an international city that it is possible to buy every conceivable type of bread, from fresh sourdough Poilâne bread at Poilâne on Elizabeth Street to rosemary, raisin, or sea salt bread at & Clarke's on Kensington Church Street. The bakeries reflect the city's extraordinary ethnic diversity, each catering to neighborhood taste by making Italian *pugliese*, Turkish flat *pide*, French *fougasse*, soft white English baps, or Jewish rye and challah. The most notable bakers experiment in a way they could not elsewhere in the world because Londoners are often happy to try anything new and are accustomed to being introduced to innovative ideas and unfamiliar ingredients.

Dan Lepard is the most talked-about baker in Britain. He has worked for some of London's foremost restaurants and chefs, including Giorgio Locatelli at Zafferano and Locanda Locatelli, and his influence has spread. His book, *The Handmade Loaf,* has positioned him at the forefront of the British bread revival. Restaurant critic Fay Maschler has described him as "the bread supremo."

Baker & Spice in Denyer Street, where Lepard once worked, is a purveyor of irresistible cakes, outstanding breads, and extraordinary pastries and tarts. Owner Gail Stephens, who is fiercely passionate about her baked goods, has rightly won critical acclaim. She sells a huge variety of breads, including a *pane con noci* that is so packed with walnuts and raisins it is almost a cake, a sensational garlic bread studded with whole caramelized cloves, and a traditional British milk knot, a small white roll with a top knot.

Restaurateur Sally Clarke's bakery, & Clarke's, prides itself on using the highest-quality ingredients—without artificial colors, preservatives, or improvers—in the fresh breads and pastries on display early each morning. Every night, the bakers hand-shape and bake more than two thousand loaves, which are sent to some of the top restaurants, shops, and hotels in central London. The inventive range includes an oatmeal honeypot with organic oats, baked in a flowerpot shape; a loaf in the form of ears of corn; and narrow breadsticks with dried figs and fennel seeds.

Legendary across the city for its diversity of handmade breads—from eastern Europe, Ireland, the Mediterranean, and the United States—De Gustibus is best known for its six-day sourdough loaf. Other temptations include pumpernickel, Polish rye, Irish wheat loaf, and tortino, a Tuscan focaccia filled with vegetables and cheese.

Artisanal bakers approach their craft with regard for both tradition and innovation.

Originally from the county of Cornwall, the Cornish pasty was first conceived as a lunchtime snack for local tin miners. The crimped edge of the pastry parcel acted as a handle and was later discarded after being blackened by the miner's fingers. So large were the pasties that one end contained a savory filling, the other a sweet one—making a complete, portable meal.

Questions of Authenticity

Bakers throughout the country make Cornish pasties, although the "authentic" method is the subject of hot debate. Classic pasties combine diced beef with onions, sliced potatoes, and root vegetables such as turnips or carrots. Some cooks claim that the order in which the ingredients are layered is crucial. Others assert that the position of the crimp—on the top or on the side—is what determines authenticity. They all agree on one point: each pasty must be made from raw ingredients.

History of the Pasty

Many Cornish folk will tell you that a genuine pasty can be made only with short pastry, while others advocate using a rough puff pastry. Either way, in times gone by, the pastry needed to be sufficiently strong to withstand a miner's descent into a mineshaft and thick enough to provide insulation for the hot filling until the miner could snatch a moment from his toil to eat. Lest his pasty be confused with another miner's, his wife would mark it with a knife, carving his initials into the left-hand side. This was especially useful when the miner wished to save a corner for later, or to placate the Knockers, the "little people" of the mines, who were thought to cause mischief.

Surprisingly for a coastal region, fish rarely found its way into the Cornish pasty. The more superstitious among the fishermen thought it bad luck even to take a pasty on board the boat, regardless of its contents. Today, the Cornish pasty has joined the fast-food brigade, with fillings as outré as crab, pork and apple, lamb and mint, cheese and bacon—even chicken balti, a spicy Indian curry.

Making Cornish Pasties

MAKING THE PASTRY First, flour and salt are sifted into a bowl. Traditionally, lard is then rubbed into the flour until the mixture resembles fine bread crumbs. Ice-cold water is then added little by little to make a soft dough. The dough is then chilled.

MAKING THE FILLING Beef is the traditional filling for pasties. It is first trimmed, then finely chopped (never ground). Finely sliced potatoes, diced onions, and root vegetables, such as carrots, rutabagas, or turnips, are then added to the beef along with chopped fresh thyme, salt, and pepper.

FORMING THE PASTIES The pastry is rolled out, and cut into rounds. The filling is then arranged down the center of each round, and the rim is brushed with beaten egg. The opposite sides of the round are folded over the top of the filling and crimped together to form a wavy seam. The pasties are then brushed with egg.

BAKING THE PASTIES The pasties are baked in a 400°F (200°C) oven for 20 minutes. The heat is then reduced to 350°F (180°C), and they are baked until golden brown, 40 minutes longer.

AFTERNOON TEA

The scent of Earl Grey tea and a plate of warm buttered

scones anticipate one of London's much-loved pleasures.

While the formalities of tea are observed in some elegant hotels, most Londoners approach this centuries-old ritual with a relaxed attitude suited to the demands of urban life. Nevertheless, traditional savories such as scones flecked with ham and artisanal cheese and delicate egg sandwiches spiced with cress are still welcome accompaniments to freshly brewed tea. Classic mince pies and contemporary versions of fairy cakes are among the delicious array of cakes on tea menus. Nowadays, the beverage of choice might be a cup of coffee, enjoyed in one of the city's many cafés with a slice of drizzle cake.

CHOCOLATE FAIRY CAKES

Fairy cakes have been enjoying a renaissance in recent years. Instead of buying a large cake to celebrate a birthday or an anniversary, Londoners opt for these diminutive cakes, whether vanilla, almond, lemon, orange, or chocolate sponge, covered with icing and usually decorated with candied organic flower petals or even wisps of edible gold leaf. Traditionally, such cakes are served for tea or with morning coffee. London mothers bake vast quantities to sell at school fêtes; the competition ensures a beautiful presentation.

1 Preheat the oven to 325°F (165°C). Line 24 mini-muffin cups with paper liners or grease with butter.

2 In a small saucepan, combine the chocolate, milk, and half of the brown sugar. Set over low heat and stir constantly until the chocolate is melted. Remove from the heat and stir in the ground espresso. Set aside to cool.

3 In a bowl, using an electric mixer on medium speed, beat the butter and remaining brown sugar until light and fluffy, about 5 minutes. Add the egg and beat until incorporated. In a separate bowl, sift the flour, baking powder, and cocoa powder. Add to the butter mixture and beat until incorporated, about 2 minutes. Using a metal spoon, fold in the cooled chocolate mixture. Divide the batter among the mini-muffin cups. Bake until a skewer inserted in the center of a cake comes out clean, 15–20 minutes. Remove from the oven and transfer to a wire rack to cool.

4 To make the icing, combine the butter, chocolate, and corn syrup in a bowl set over, but not touching, a pan of simmering water. Stir constantly until the mixture forms a smooth paste, about 5 minutes. Set aside until cool. Using an electric mixer on high speed, beat until the mixture forms a thick, fluffy icing.

5 Spread the top of each cake with a thick layer of icing. Let set for one hour before serving. If desired, garnish with finely grated white chocolate. Store in an airtight container at room temperature for up to 2 days.

Serve with Earl Grey or Darjeeling tea.

2 oz (60 g) dark chocolate, coarsely chopped

¼ cup (2 fl oz/60 ml) whole milk

1 cup (7 oz/220 g) plus 2 tablespoons firmly packed brown sugar

2 teaspoons very finely ground espresso

4 tablespoons (2 oz/60 g) unsalted butter, at room temperature

1 large egg, beaten

⅔ cup (4 oz/125 g) all-purpose (plain) flour

½ teaspoon baking powder

1 tablespoon Dutch-process cocoa powder

FOR THE ICING

½ cup (3 oz/90 g) unsalted butter

2½ oz (75 g) dark chocolate, coarsely chopped

1½ teaspoons light corn syrup or golden syrup

Finely grated white chocolate (optional)

Makes 24 cakes

Chocolate Shops

Londoners have a strong sense of style, and for certain occasions only a smart box of chocolates will do. Charbonnel et Walker and Fortnum & Mason were the best choices for years, the former supplying the royal family since 1875. Charbonnel's became famous for its chocolate-dipped violet and rose creams.

For years, nothing challenged the old order in Britain. Then, in 1983, Chantal Coady opened Rococo, a glamorous chocolate boutique. She was passionate about selling the finest chocolate: white truffles infused with cardamom and chocolate bars flavored with delicacies such as geranium and sea salt.

In 2000, L'Artisan du Chocolat set up a modest stall at Borough Market and started to sell handmade couture chocolates. Rather than containing traditional chocolate flavorings found in France, the ganaches were infused with innovative ingredients such as black cardamom and Moroccan mint. The company started supplying top British chefs such as Gordon Ramsay before opening a shop. Londoners can now slip into the chic environment whenever they need to savor a rosemary or red wine chocolate.

HOT CROSS BUNS

Every Good Friday in the nineteenth century, cries of "one-a-penny, two-a-penny, hot cross buns" reverberated around the streets of London as vendors sold sweet buns marked with a cross. The spicy fruited buns originated in Tudor times, and by the reign of Elizabeth I they were so popular that their sale was restricted to the serious observances of burials, Christmas, and Good Friday. What fed their appeal was Londoners' taste for expensive imports such as sugar, spices, and dried fruits. Today, hot cross buns are eaten throughout much of the year, for breakfast or tea, or as a snack.

½ cup (4 fl oz/125 ml) whole milk

2 cups (10 oz/315 g) bread flour, or as needed

2 tablespoons superfine (caster) sugar

½ teaspoon *each* fine sea salt and ground cinnamon

¼ teaspoon *each* ground mace and freshly grated nutmeg

⅛ teaspoon *each* ground cloves and ground allspice (optional)

1½ tablespoons cold unsalted butter, diced

1 teaspoon rapid-rise yeast

⅓ cup (2 oz/60 g) *each* dried currants, golden raisins (sultanas), and mixed candied citrus peel

1 large egg, beaten

FOR THE PASTRY CROSSES

⅓ cup (2 oz/60 g) all-purpose (plain) flour

1 tablespoon unsalted butter, diced

1 teaspoon superfine (caster) sugar

FOR THE GLAZE

2 tablespoons whole milk

1½ tablespoons granulated sugar

Makes 6 buns

1 In a small saucepan, warm the milk to 105°F (40°C). Remove from the heat and set aside.

2 Sift the 2 cups bread flour into a large bowl. Stir in the superfine sugar, salt, cinnamon, mace, nutmeg, cloves, and allspice (if using). Using your fingertips, rub the butter into the flour until the mixture forms crumbs the size of fine bread crumbs. Mix in the yeast and then the currants, raisins, and candied peel. Make a well in the center and stir in the egg and enough of the reserved milk to form a soft dough. It should not be too sticky; if it clings to your fingers, add a little more flour.

3 Turn the dough out onto a lightly floured work surface. Knead thoroughly until smooth and elastic, about 10 minutes. Return the dough to the bowl, cover with plastic wrap, and let stand in a warm place until the dough has risen by a third, 3–5 hours. The timing depends on the temperature of the kitchen.

4 Lightly oil a baking sheet. Turn the risen dough out onto a lightly floured work surface. Knead for 1 minute, then divide into 6 equal pieces. Shape each piece into a neat ball and place on the prepared baking sheet, flattening each ball slightly. Cover lightly with plastic wrap and set aside until the dough is very puffy, about 45 minutes.

5 Preheat the oven to 400°F (200°C). To make the pastry crosses, sift the all-purpose flour into a small bowl. Using your fingertips, rub in the butter until the mixture forms fine crumbs. Mix in the superfine sugar. Stir in 1 tablespoon cold water to make a firm dough. Turn the dough out onto a lightly floured work surface and roll into a rectangle about 8 inches (20 cm) by 2 inches (5 cm) and ⅛ inch (3 mm) thick. Cut the pastry into 12 strips, each about 4 inches (10 cm) long and ¼ inch (6 mm) wide. For each bun, brush 2 strips with a little water and arrange, brushed side down, in a cross on the top of the bun. Bake until golden brown, about 15 minutes.

6 Meanwhile, make the glaze: In a small saucepan over low heat, combine the milk and granulated sugar and cook, stirring occasionally, until the sugar is dissolved, about 5 minutes. Raise the heat to high and boil vigorously until the glaze becomes syrupy, about 30 seconds.

7 When the buns are done, transfer to a wire rack and immediately brush with the hot glaze. Serve the buns warm or at room temperature. They can also be split open and toasted.

Serve with Assam or Darjeeling tea or coffee.

Note: The buns can be wrapped tightly with plastic wrap and frozen for up to 1 month. Before serving, bring the buns to room temperature, about 1 hour. Preheat the oven to 350°F (180°C), place the buns on a baking sheet, and warm through, 4–5 minutes.

EGG AND CRESS SANDWICHES

Tea was first served in Britain in 1658 at the Sultaness Head, a coffeehouse in Sweetings Rents near London's Royal Exchange. One hundred years passed before afternoon tea became established. It initially featured thin, buttered slices of bread, but by the nineteenth century, the centerpiece was dainty sandwiches filled with eggs, cucumber, or watercress. Peppery, small-leaved cresses, including watercress, are members of the mustard family. Garden cress, which is often sold at farmers' markets, can be used in these sandwiches.

1 Bring a small saucepan two-thirds full of water to a boil over medium-high heat. Carefully lower the eggs into the water, return the water to a boil, and boil the eggs for 10 minutes. Immediately plunge the eggs into ice water. When the eggs are cool enough to handle, peel each egg under cold running water, being sure to remove every speck of eggshell. Pat the eggs dry with a kitchen towel.

2 Place the eggs in a bowl and finely mash with a fork or potato masher. Add the mayonnaise and mash again. Season to taste with salt, black pepper, and cayenne.

3 Spread 2 slices of bread with the egg mixture, dividing it evenly. Arrange the cress on top of the egg mixture. Top with the remaining bread slices, pressing firmly. Using a serrated knife, remove the crusts from each sandwich, then cut into 3 fingers or 4 triangles.

4 If not serving the sandwiches immediately, cover tightly with plastic wrap and refrigerate for up to 2 hours.

Serve with Darjeeling or Earl Grey tea.

2 large eggs

1 tablespoon mayonnaise

Fine sea salt and freshly ground black pepper

Pinch of cayenne pepper, or to taste

4 slices good-quality, thinly sliced white bread

½ cup (½ oz/15 g) mustard cress, garden cress, or trimmed watercress sprigs

Makes 2 servings

The Sandwich

For the last 150 years, sandwiches have fueled Londoners' workdays. At lunchtime, office workers pour into cafés to buy their favorite "saunnie." Classic fillings such as smoked salmon or cheese and pickle are still popular. Among recent trends are sandwiches with Thai chicken or shrimp (prawns) and arugula (rocket).

John Montagu, fourth Earl of Sandwich, is said to have invented the sandwich around 1760 while gambling. Keen not to be distracted from his game, he ordered cold beef served between slices of buttered bread. Within two years, the fashionable elite were eating "the Sandwich." By the mid-1800s, its consumption had spread throughout London society. Watercress sandwiches were served for breakfast, cucumber for tea, and jam at picnics. Theater patrons bought ham and mustard sandwiches from street vendors, and the wealthy dined on dainty veal sandwiches.

Sandwiches have always invited experimentation, but few rivaled Mrs. Sawbridge's creation two hundred years ago. She made and then scornfully ate a delicate sandwich containing a hundred-pound note given her by an admirer.

CHEESE AND HAM SCONES

A proper afternoon tea can still be sampled in most of London's grand hotels, such as the elegant Palm Court at the Ritz and the wood-paneled Drawing Room at the Connaught in Mayfair. It always includes a savory dish or two, for example, sandwiches, anchovy toasts, crumpets, or scones. Although scones are commonly sweet, studded with golden raisins (sultanas), and served with clotted cream, many savory varieties exist, one of the most popular being cheese and ham. The best Cheddar, tangy, nutty, and rich, is made by small artisanal dairies such as Keen's or Montgomery's in Somerset.

1¾ cups (9 oz/280 g) all-purpose (plain) flour

1 teaspoon cream of tartar

½ teaspoon baking soda (bicarbonate of soda)

Pinch of fine sea salt

4 tablespoons (2 oz/60 g) cold unsalted butter, diced, plus more for serving

¾ cup (3 oz/90 g) finely grated mature Cheddar cheese

⅔ cup (4 oz/125 g) finely diced ham

⅔ cup (5 fl oz/160 ml) whole milk

1 large egg

Makes 12 scones

1 Preheat the oven to 425°F (220°C). Lightly oil a baking sheet.

2 Sift the flour, cream of tartar, baking soda, and salt into a bowl. Using a pastry blender or 2 knives, cut in the 4 tablespoons butter until the mixture forms coarse crumbs. Alternatively, place the sifted dry ingredients in a food processor, add the 4 tablespoons butter, and pulse 4 or 5 times until the mixture forms coarse crumbs; return to the bowl. Using a fork, stir in the cheese and ham. In a small bowl, beat the milk into the egg, then add to the flour mixture. Stir just until a rough, soft dough forms.

3 Turn the dough out onto a floured work surface and lightly knead until it clings together and is soft and puffy, about 1 minute. Gently roll out into a round about ¾ inch (2 cm) thick. Dust a 2¼-inch (5.5-cm) round biscuit cutter with flour and, using a quick, sharp motion, cut out scones as close together as possible. Gather the scraps of dough, knead briefly, roll out, and cut additional scones. Place the scones 1½ inches (4 cm) apart on the prepared baking sheet.

4 Bake until the scones are golden brown, about 10 minutes. Serve hot or let cool to room temperature on a wire rack. Serve with butter. The scones should be eaten the same day they are baked, or can be frozen for up to 2 weeks in an airtight container.

Serve with Darjeeling, Earl Grey, or Lapsang Souchong tea.

LEMON-LAVENDER DRIZZLE CAKE

Londoners like nothing better than lingering in a café over coffee or tea and cake, while watching the world pass by. Midmorning and midafternoon are their favorite times for such indulgences, and many cafés offer outdoor seating much of the year. While some Londoners prefer French confections, others are fond of simple English cakes like this lavender cake with the fresh, floral taste of the English countryside, embellished with an old-fashioned drizzle icing. The best source for pesticide-free lavender is your own garden or a friend's.

1 Preheat the oven to 350°F (180°C). Generously butter a 9-by-5-inch (23-by-13-cm) loaf pan.

2 Strip the flowers from the lavender sprigs. Place in a food processor and add the superfine sugar, butter, lemon zest, and salt. Process until pale and fluffy, 2–3 minutes. Transfer to a large bowl. Add the eggs one at a time alternately with one-fourth of the flour, beating well with a wooden spoon after each addition. Gently stir in the ground almonds and the lemon juice.

3 Spoon the batter into the prepared pan and smooth the top. Bake for 10 minutes. Reduce the oven temperature to 325°F (165°C) and bake until a skewer inserted into the center comes out clean, 50–55 minutes. Remove from the oven and let rest in the pan on a wire rack for 5 minutes. Run a table knife around the edge of the pan and turn the cake out onto the rack. Place right side up and let cool.

4 Meanwhile, make the icing: Sift the confectioner's sugar into a bowl. Using a wooden spoon, stir in the lemon juice, a few drops at a time. The icing should be thick but spreadable. If the icing is too stiff, add a few more drops of lemon juice.

5 Using a knife and dipping it in hot water if it becomes too sticky, spread the icing over the top of the cooled cake, making sure that it drips down the sides. Let the cake stand until the icing is set, about 1 hour. Decorate with fresh lavender flowers, if desired, placing them on top of the icing. The cake will keep, stored in an airtight container without the flower garnish, for up to 3 days.

8 sprigs pesticide-free fresh lavender flowers (see note) or 1 teaspoon finely chopped, pesticide-free fresh lavender leaves, plus flowers for serving (optional)

1¼ cups (9 oz/280 g) superfine (caster) sugar

1 cup (8 oz/250 g) unsalted butter, at room temperature

Finely grated zest of 2 lemons

Pinch of fine sea salt

4 large eggs

½ cup (2 oz/60 g) sifted all-purpose (plain) flour

1½ cups (6 oz/185 g) blanched, ground almonds

¼ cup (2 fl oz/60 ml) fresh lemon juice

FOR THE ICING

1½ cups (6 oz/185 g) confectioner's (icing) sugar

Juice of ½ large lemon, or as needed

Makes 8–10 servings

London Coffeehouses

A love of good coffee helped shape modern London. In the early seventeenth century, British travelers to Turkey developed such a liking for arabica coffee beans that they imported them on their return. The craze for coffee soon took hold of fashionable society, and in 1652 the first of the city's coffeehouses was opened on St. Michael's Alley by Pasqua Rosee, a Croatian native. At their peak there were hundreds of coffeehouses in London, and the coffeehouse became a place where men of all classes could meet, talk, and circulate uncensored news sheets. Business deals discussed over coffee created Lloyd's of London insurance company, and some of the city's most exclusive gentleman's clubs are direct descendants of coffeehouses.

After two hundred years, coffeehouses began to decline, partly because they became quite popular with characters of ill repute and partly because tea had superseded coffee in popularity. Tea, grown in the British colonies, was less expensive than coffee. Today, however, coffee is more popular than ever, and you can find cafés and coffee shops on nearly every street corner.

MINCE PIES

A centuries-old British specialty, mince pies appear in London shops about six weeks before Christmas. The small pies take their name from the filling, a preserve called mincemeat. In medieval times, the mixture of dried fruits, candied peels, and apples also contained beef. Suet, which later took the place of beef, can be omitted from contemporary versions, like the one here. This recipe makes more mincemeat than you will need for the pies. Since its flavor improves with age, the extra can be canned for future use. The pies are served with mulled wine for festive occasions or eaten with sandwiches and cake at tea.

FOR THE MINCEMEAT

2 lb (1 kg) tart green apples

¾ cup (6 fl oz/180 ml) hard apple cider

1 cup (7 oz/220 g) firmly packed dark brown sugar

1½ cups (9 oz/280 g) *each* dried currants and raisins

⅓ cup (2 oz/60 g) glacé cherries, roughly chopped (see page 186)

Grated zest and juice of 1 lemon and 1 orange

½ teaspoon ground cinnamon

Pinch of freshly grated nutmeg

Small pinch of ground cloves

¼ cup (2 fl oz/60 ml) brandy

FOR THE PASTRY

1½ cups (7½ oz/235 g) all-purpose (plain) flour

Pinch of fine sea salt

⅓ cup (3 oz/90 g) cold unsalted butter, diced

1 large egg yolk

3–4 tablespoons cold water

1 tablespoon whole milk

2 tablespoons granulated sugar

Makes 12 mince pies

1 To make the mincemeat, peel, core, and shred the apples. In a large nonreactive saucepan over medium heat, combine the cider and brown sugar and cook, stirring occasionally, until the sugar is dissolved. Add the apples, currants, raisins, cherries, lemon and orange zest and juice, cinnamon, nutmeg, and cloves. Cook, stirring constantly, until the mixture comes slowly to a boil, about 5 minutes. Reduce the heat to low, cover partially, and simmer gently until the mixture forms a thick, soft paste, about 1 hour. Uncover, raise the heat to medium, and cook briskly, stirring frequently, until all the liquid has evaporated, about 10 minutes. Stir in the brandy. If not using the mincemeat immediately, store in sterilized jars.

2 To sterilize jars, while the mincemeat is cooking, preheat the oven to 125°F (52°C). Wash four 1-cup (8–fl oz/250-ml) glass jam jars in warm soapy water, rinse in clean warm water, and set in the oven to dry. Spoon the hot mincemeat into the sterilized jars to within ¼ inch (6 mm) of the tops. Wipe the rims clean with a hot, damp kitchen towel, top with metal canning lids, and seal tightly with screw bands. Process in a boiling-water bath for 15 minutes. Using tongs, transfer the jars to a kitchen towel and let cool. Store in a cool, dark place. The mincemeat will keep for up to 6 months.

3 To make the pastry, sift the flour and salt into a bowl. Using a pastry blender or 2 knives, cut in the butter until the mixture forms coarse crumbs. Alternatively, place the sifted dry ingredients in a food processor, add the butter, and pulse 4 or 5 times until the mixture forms coarse crumbs; return to the bowl.

Using a fork, stir in the egg yolk and enough of the cold water to form a rough dough. Turn the dough out onto a lightly floured work surface and lightly knead until smooth, about 1 minute. Shape the dough into a disk ¾ inch (2 cm) thick, wrap in plastic wrap, and refrigerate for at least 30 minutes or up to 12 hours.

4 Preheat the oven to 350°F (180°C). Lightly butter 12 tartlet pans about 2½ inches (6 cm) in diameter. On a lightly floured work surface, roll out two-thirds of the dough into a round ⅛ inch (3 mm) thick. Using a 3-inch (7.5-cm) cookie cutter, cut out 12 circles. Gather the scraps of dough and roll out with the remaining dough, dusting the dough with flour as needed to keep it from sticking to the work surface. Using a 2½-inch (6-cm) round or star-shaped cookie cutter, cut out 12 shapes. Line each prepared pie pan with a large circle of dough. Fill with about 3 teaspoons of mincemeat. Brush the edges of a small pastry circle with milk, place milk side down on top of the filling, and press the edges together lightly to seal. If using stars, brush the tips of the stars with milk, place on top of the filling, and press the tips into the edges to seal. Prick the top of each pie with a sharp knife, then brush with milk and sprinkle with granulated sugar.

5 Bake the pies until the crusts are golden, about 20 minutes. Remove from the pans and let cool on a wire rack. Serve warm or at room temperature. The pies can be stored in an airtight tin for 2 days.

Serve with mulled wine or Darjeeling or Earl Grey tea.

STARTERS

Global influences and a taste for innovation are the foundation fo

appetizers on both restaurant menus and the tables of home cooks.

Londoners like to experiment when making
starters and canapés. The distinctive flavors of
cuisines from around the world are married with
local ingredients to make Thai meatballs with
a sweet chile-lemongrass sauce or a Middle
Eastern meze plate with hummus, tabbouleh,
and crisp vegetables. At parties, elegant blini
with smoked salmon and crème fraîche, colorful
vegetable crisps, or spicy samosas might be
passed around to guests. Restaurant diners
regularly order an appetizer or two in place of
a main course, and home cooks might prepare a
savory cheese tart with a salad for a light lunch.

BLINI WITH SMOKED SALMON AND CRÈME FRAÎCHE

Blini with smoked salmon or caviar have long been popular in the City of London, the capital's prosperous financial district. The area, a mere square mile, is renowned for its expensive tastes, which often influence chefs working elsewhere in the capital. Blini, for example, are now regularly found on menus throughout London. Buckwheat flour adds a distinctive nutty taste to the pancakes, but since it can be hard to find, it can be replaced with whole-wheat (wholemeal) flour. Some of the finest smoked salmon comes from Scotland and Ireland, where wild Atlantic salmon is skillfully smoked to bring out its sweet flavor.

1 To make the blini, warm a large bowl by filling it with hot water, draining it, and wiping it dry. In the bowl, combine the all-purpose and buckwheat flours and yeast. In a small saucepan over medium heat, warm the milk just until small bubbles appear along the edge of the pan, but do not let it come to a boil. Slowly pour the milk into the dry ingredients, beating constantly with a wooden spoon to form a smooth batter. Cover with plastic wrap and let rise in a warm place until doubled in bulk, about 2 hours.

2 In a bowl, beat together the egg yolk, salt, melted butter, and sour cream. Add to the risen batter and, using the wooden spoon, beat until combined. In a bowl, whisk the egg white until stiff peaks form. Using a metal spoon, fold into the batter. Cover with plastic wrap and let stand for 30 minutes.

3 Preheat the oven to 125°F (52°C). In a large nonstick frying pan over medium-high heat, warm 1 teaspoon of the sunflower oil. When it is hot, working in batches, drop tablespoonfuls of batter into the pan, allowing 1½ inches (4 cm) between each blini. Cook

until the blini are puffed and golden brown and tiny bubbles appear on the surface, about 2 minutes. Using a palette knife or a spatula, turn the blini and cook until golden brown, about 2 minutes. Transfer to an ovenproof plate and keep warm in the oven. Repeat the process, using 1 teaspoon of oil for each batch of blini. You should have about 16 blini.

4 Divide the blini among individual plates. To serve, place a heaping tablespoonful of crème fraîche on each plate, setting it partially on the warm blini. Divide the salmon among the plates, setting it atop the blini. Garnish each plate with chives, a light grinding of pepper (if using), and a lemon wedge. Serve at once.

Serve with a creamy white Burgundy or Blanc des Blancs Champagne.

FOR THE BLINI

½ cup (2½ oz/75 g) all-purpose (plain) flour

¼ cup (1½ oz/45 g) buckwheat flour

½ teaspoon rapid-rise yeast

½ cup (4 fl oz/125 ml) whole milk

1 large egg, separated

Pinch of fine sea salt

1 tablespoon unsalted butter, melted

1 tablespoon sour cream

4 teaspoons sunflower oil or clarified unsalted butter (see page 185)

FOR SERVING

¾ cup (6 oz/185 g) crème fraîche

13 oz (410 g) thinly sliced smoked salmon

6 chives, coarsely snipped

Freshly ground pepper (optional)

4 lemon wedges

Makes 4 servings

POTTED SHRIMP

Potted shrimp is traditionally made with indigenous tiny, sweet brown shrimp measuring only 2½ inches (6 cm) from head to tail, but larger shrimp, cut into small pieces, may also be used. This recipe follows the eighteenth-century method of seasoning the shelled shrimps with ground mace and cayenne pepper and simmering them very gently in butter before sealing them in little china pots, replaced here by ramekins. Londoners like to eat potted shrimp in classic British restaurants, such as Simpson's-in-the-Strand or the Paternoster Chop House in Paternoster Square.

1¾ cup (14 oz/440 g) unsalted butter, clarified (see page 185)

1 lb (500 g) cooked, shelled, small or medium shrimp (prawns)

¼ teaspoon ground mace

¼ teaspoon cayenne pepper

Buttered hot toast for serving

2 lemons, cut into wedges, for serving

6 chives, coarsely snipped, for serving (optional)

Makes 4 servings

1 Pour 1 cup (8 fl oz/250 ml) of the clarified butter into a small nonreactive saucepan. Reserve the remaining butter. Pat the shrimp dry with paper towels. Remove any tiny pieces of shell clinging to them. Cut the shrimp into ¼-inch (6-mm) pieces. Add the shrimp, mace, and cayenne to the butter in the saucepan. Set over low heat. If the shrimp are cold, the butter will thicken. Stir until the butter melts, then very gently cook until the shrimp are hot and the spices have infused into the butter, about 5 minutes.

2 Divide the shrimp and the butter mixture among ¼-cup (2–fl oz/60-ml) ramekins, firmly pressing down on the shrimp with a metal spoon. Refrigerate until the butter is set, about 4 hours.

3 In the small saucepan over low heat, warm the remaining clarified butter just until it melts, but before it becomes hot. Pour the butter into the ramekins, dividing evenly. Refrigerate until cold and set, about 2 hours or up to overnight.

4 Serve the potted shrimp with warm toast and lemon wedges. Garnish with the chives, if desired.

Serve with a buttery white Burgundy such as Chassagne-Montrachet or Pouilly-Fuissé.

Note: If you allow the potted shrimp to set overnight, the flavors of the dish will become more developed. This dish should be eaten no later than 1 day after it is made.

VEGETABLE CRISPS

Having a drink after work is integral to London life. Most Londoners head to a local pub or bar for a few hours of socializing before dinner. Salty snacks are an essential accompaniment to such evenings. Most pubs sell packets of crisps or nuts, but stylish bars serve their own vegetable crisps, bread sticks, and marinated olives. The crisps are made from finely sliced root vegetables, such as potatoes, parsnips, and celery root, then are tossed in fine sea salt, but they can also be flavored with a dusting of chili powder or chopped fresh thyme.

1 Using a mandoline or sharp knife, cut the parsnip lengthwise into slices slightly thinner than a coin. As you cut the slices, place them in a bowl of water. Repeat for the potato, celery root, and beet, placing the slices of each vegetable into separate bowls of water. Set aside to soak for 20 minutes to remove the excess starch.

2 In a large, heavy frying pan over medium-high heat, pour in enough sunflower oil to reach a depth of 4 inches (10 cm). Heat to 375°F (190°C) on a deep-frying thermometer. Drain the vegetable slices and pat dry with paper towels or a clean kitchen towel. Carefully place a handful of parsnip slices in the hot oil and fry until golden and crisp, about 3 minutes. Transfer to a wire rack lined with paper towels to drain. When the oil returns to 375°F (190°C), fry the remaining parsnip slices. Cook the potato slices, then the celery root slices, and finally the beet slices in the same way, letting the oil return to 375°F (190°C) before adding each batch to the pan. The potato slices will cook in 3 minutes; the celery root and beet slices will cook in 4 minutes and will crinkle slightly and not become crisp until they begin to cool.

3 Place the crisps in a bowl and season to taste with salt. Serve at once.

Serve with cocktails or a glass of berry-scented rosé from Provence.

1 large parsnip, peeled

1 russet potato, peeled

1 small celery root (celeriac), peeled and halved lengthwise

1 large red beet, peeled

Sunflower oil for deep-frying

Fine sea salt

Makes 6 servings

London Gin

Gin, distilled from corn or barley and flavored with juniper berries and other aromatics, has been associated with London since the Protestant William of Orange from Holland took over the throne from the Catholic King James II in 1688. Drinking Jenever, the early Dutch gin, became a symbol of Protestant patriotism. Parliament banned the French import of wine and brandy from Catholic France and encouraged the wholesale distillation of gin. British distillers began to make huge quantities of the cheap and lethally strong drink, which was consumed by the poor and working class. In the mid-eighteenth century, production of domestic gin was reformed. Shortly thereafter, some of the great London gin distillers emerged: Philip Booth in Clerkenwell (1778), Alexander Gordon in Clerkenwell (1786), Charles Tanqueray in Bloomsbury (1830), and James Burroughs in Chelsea (1863), known for Beefeater gin. They developed what became known as the London style of gin, using pure water from outlying villages and a continuous still to produce a light, dry gin that remains popular today.

SPICY THAI MEATBALLS WITH CHILE-LEMONGRASS SAUCE

When Thai restaurants first appeared in London in the 1970s, the combination of hot spices and Chinese cooking methods immediately appealed to Londoners, who soon incorporated the cuisine into their culinary repertoire. Local markets responded by starting to carry curry paste, fish sauce, kaffir lime leaves, coconut milk, fresh lemongrass, and other essential ingredients. As cooks experimented, they varied or simplified Thai dishes such as these meatballs, which are served here as canapés on lettuce leaves, accompanied by an aromatic dipping sauce. The recipe can easily be doubled for a large party.

FOR THE SAUCE

1 lemongrass stalk

2 tablespoons sugar

½ teaspoon red pepper flakes

¼ cup (2 fl oz/60 ml) boiling water

2½ tablespoons white wine vinegar

FOR THE MEATBALLS

½ bunch fresh cilantro (fresh coriander), including stems, finely chopped

2 green (spring) onions, white and pale green parts only, finely chopped

1 clove garlic, finely chopped

Finely grated zest of 1 lemon

Finely ground black pepper

Pinch of freshly grated nutmeg

½ large egg, lightly beaten

1½ teaspoons Thai fish sauce

6 oz (185 g) ground (minced) pork

All-purpose (plain) flour for coating

3 tablespoons sunflower oil

16 small Bibb lettuce leaves

Makes 6–8 servings

1 To make the sauce, trim off the upper leafy part of the lemongrass stalk and the tough end of the bulb. Remove the tough outer layer of the stalk. Finely slice the stalk and place in a small bowl with the sugar and red pepper flakes. Add the boiling water and stir until the sugar is dissolved, about 2 minutes. Stir in the vinegar. Pour the sauce into a dipping bowl and set on a serving platter large enough to hold the lettuce leaves in a single layer.

2 To make the meatballs, combine the cilantro, green onions, garlic, lemon zest, ⅛ teaspoon black pepper, nutmeg, egg, and fish sauce in a food processor. Pulse 4 or 5 times until puréed. Add the pork and pulse 2 or 3 times in short bursts until the mixture is minced. Do not overprocess the mixture, or it will have a gummy texture.

3 Place a generous amount of flour on a dinner plate. Dip your hands in the flour, pick up a small walnut-sized piece of the pork mixture, dust it with flour, and lightly shape into a ball. Set aside on a plate. Repeat to make a total of 16 balls.

4 Preheat the oven to 400°F (200°C). In a nonstick frying pan over medium-low heat, heat the oil. When the oil is hot but not smoking, gently add the meatballs and cook, turning as needed, until uniformly lightly browned, about 4 minutes. Transfer to a plate lined with paper towels to drain. (The meatballs can be refrigerated for up to 24 hours before proceeding.)

5 Place the meatballs on a rimmed baking sheet, cover with aluminum foil, and bake until cooked through and hot, about 20 minutes. Arrange the lettuce leaves on the serving platter. Place a meatball on each lettuce leaf and serve with the sauce for spooning over the meatballs.

Serve with a light Thai beer such as Singha or a citrusy white wine such as an Austrian Grüner Veltliner or a dry German Riesling.

STILTON AND LEEK TART

Stilton cheese became famous in 1740 when Frances Paulet supplied Cooper Thornhill, owner of Bell Inn at Stilton, with her large rounds of nutty-tasting, blue-veined cow's milk cheese. The inn was a day's journey by coach from London on the Great North Road, and soon Thornhill was sending coach-loads of her excellent cheese to the capital. Stilton, still made in Nottinghamshire, Leicestershire, and Derbyshire, remains a favorite cheese. At Christmas, London cheesemongers display towering piles of mature truckles. Customers purchase half truckles to eat over the holidays, adding leftovers to soups, salads, and tarts.

1 To make the pastry, combine the flour and salt in a medium bowl. Using a pastry blender or 2 knives, cut in the butter until the mixture forms coarse crumbs. Alternatively, place the flour and salt in a food processor, add the butter, and pulse 4 or 5 times until the mixture forms coarse crumbs; transfer to a bowl. Using a fork, stir in enough of the cold water to form a rough dough. Turn the dough out onto a lightly floured work surface and lightly knead just until smooth, about 30 seconds. Shape the dough into a disk ¾ inch (2 cm) thick, wrap tightly in plastic wrap, and refrigerate for at least 30 minutes or up to overnight.

2 On a lightly floured work surface, roll out the dough into an evenly thick round large enough to cover the bottom and sides of a 9-inch (23-cm) tart pan with a removable bottom. It should be about 10 inches (25 cm) in diameter. Drape the dough over the rolling pin and ease into the tart pan, pressing it into place. If there is an overhang, roll the rolling pin across the rim of the pan to remove it. Prick the dough with a fork in several places, line with parchment (baking) paper, and fill with dried beans or pie weights. Refrigerate for 30 minutes.

3 Preheat the oven to 400°F (200°C). Bake the tart shell until the pastry looks dry but is not colored, about 15 minutes. Carefully remove the paper and beans. Set the tart shell aside. Reduce the oven temperature to 350°F (180°C).

4 Meanwhile, make the filling: Remove any tough outer leaves from the leeks. Cut each leek in half lengthwise and rinse thoroughly. Trim away the dark green leaves. Thinly slice the white and pale green parts of the leeks and drain thoroughly. In a frying pan over medium heat, warm the sunflower oil. Add the leeks and cook, stirring occasionally, until wilted, about 4 minutes. Transfer to a small bowl.

5 Place the cheese, whole egg, and egg yolk in a food processor and purée until smooth. Transfer to a bowl and stir in the cream. Add the leeks and stir to combine. Season with salt and pepper. Pour into the tart shell. Bake until the filling is golden brown and just set, about 25 minutes. Serve the tart warm or at room temperature, cut into wedges.

Serve with a cassis-scented, medium-bodied red Bordeaux such as Pauillac.

FOR THE PASTRY

1½ cups (7½ oz/235 g) all-purpose (plain) flour

Fine sea salt

½ cup (4 oz/125 g) cold unsalted butter, diced

3–4 tablespoons cold water

FOR THE FILLING

5 small leeks

3 tablespoons sunflower oil

3 oz (90 g) Stilton cheese or other strong blue cheese

1 large egg, plus 1 large egg yolk

½ cup (4 fl oz/125 ml) heavy (double) cream

Fine sea salt and freshly ground pepper

Makes 6 servings

PEA AND POTATO SAMOSAS

Golden, flaky samosas, piled on deli counters across London, tempt shoppers into indulging in a deli-cious spicy snack. The fillings vary but are generally either minced lamb and peas or diced potato and peas. At Indian restaurants, samosas are an appetizer, usually accompanied with a mildly spiced mint, cilantro, or tamarind relish or a fruit chutney, such as mango. They are easy to make at home and can be served piping hot as a snack or for tea, along with traditional Indian sweets. Amchoor powder, made from ground dried green mangoes, has a fruity, sour taste. It can be found at well-stocked Indian markets.

FOR THE FILLING

½ lb (250 g) new potatoes

2 tablespoons coarsely chopped fresh cilantro (fresh coriander)

1½ tablespoons sunflower oil

½ small yellow onion, finely diced

1 small fresh green chile such as serrano, or to taste, finely chopped

½ teaspoon peeled and finely chopped fresh ginger

½ teaspoon cumin seeds

½ cup (2½ oz/75 g) fresh or frozen English peas

2 teaspoons amchoor powder or fresh lemon juice (see note)

½ teaspoon garam masala

Fine sea salt

FOR THE PASTRY

1 cup (5 oz/155 g) all-purpose (plain) flour

¼ teaspoon fine sea salt

1 tablespoon unsalted butter, melted

¼ cup (2 oz/60 g) plain yogurt, plus 1 tablespoon

Sunflower oil for deep-frying

Makes 4–6 servings

1 To make the filling, place the unpeeled potatoes in a medium saucepan with water to cover generously. Bring to a boil over medium-high heat and cook until tender, 25 minutes. Drain. When the potatoes are cool enough to handle, peel and cut into ¼-inch (6-mm) cubes. In a bowl, combine the potatoes and cilantro.

2 Meanwhile, in a small nonreactive saucepan over medium-low heat, warm the sunflower oil. Add the onion, chile, ginger, and cumin seeds and cook, stirring occasionally, until the onion is soft and golden, about 15 minutes. Stir in the peas and 3 tablespoons water. Increase the heat to medium, cover the saucepan, and simmer, stirring occasionally, until the peas are tender, about 8 minutes. Uncover and continue to cook until any excess moisture has evapo-rated. Stir in the amchoor powder and garam masala. Add this mixture to the potatoes and stir gently to combine. Season to taste with salt and set aside to cool while you make the pastry.

3 To make the pastry, sift the flour and salt into a bowl. In a small bowl, stir together the melted butter and 2 tablespoons warm water. Immediately add to the flour and stir to combine. Stir in the ¼ cup yogurt. Turn the pastry out onto a lightly floured work surface and knead until it forms a stiff but pliable dough, about 5 minutes. Divide into 6 equal pieces.

4 Working with 1 piece of dough at a time, roll it in the palm of your hand to form a round ball, dust with flour, and place on a work surface. Using a rolling pin, roll the pastry into a thin disk about 6 inches (15 cm) in diameter. Cut the pastry disk in half to make 2 semicircles and brush the edges with some of the 1 tablespoon yogurt. Place a spoonful of filling on one half of each semicircle. Fold the pastry over the filling to form a triangle. Pinch the edges to seal each samosa. Repeat to make a total of 12 samosas.

5 In a large, heavy frying pan over medium-high heat, pour in enough sunflower oil to reach a depth of 4 inches (10 cm). Heat to 375°F (190°C) on a deep-frying thermometer. Working in batches to avoid crowding, carefully add a single layer of samosas and fry until golden brown, about 4 minutes. Transfer to paper towels to drain. When the oil returns to 375°F (190°C), fry the remaining samosas.

6 Serve the samosas hot or warm with homemade or purchased Indian relish or chutney (see note).

Serve with a light Indian beer such as Kingfisher or a spicy, full-bodied white wine such as Gewürztraminer.

MEDITERRANEAN MEZE PLATE

Late into the night, particularly during the warm summer months, Londoners can imagine they are in the Middle East by strolling up and down the Marble Arch end of Edgware Road. The broad, tree-lined street is lined with Middle Eastern juice bars, restaurants, and cafés. Friends gather to enjoy the evening air, watch the world go by, and share meze—small dishes of tabbouleh, hummus, falafel, and walnut-stuffed eggplant (aubergine), along with crisp fresh vegetables and freshly baked pita bread—before moving on to kebabs or delicately spiced Iranian, Lebanese, or Egyptian stews.

1 To make the hummus, drain the chickpeas and place in a medium saucepan. Add water to cover and bring to a boil over high heat. Boil for 10 minutes, reduce the heat to medium-low, add the baking soda, and cook until the chickpeas are meltingly soft, about 50 minutes.

2 Meanwhile, make the tabbouleh: Place the bulgur wheat in a bowl with boiling water to cover and let soak for 15 minutes. Drain, rinse, and squeeze dry. Thinly slice the 3 green onions, using the white and pale green parts only. In a large bowl, combine the green onions, bulgur wheat, ⅓ cup olive oil, the juice of 1 lemon, the tomatoes, and the parsley. Season to taste with salt and pepper and transfer to a serving bowl. Set aside.

3 When the chickpeas are done, drain them, reserving the cooking water. In a food processor, purée the chickpeas and garlic until smooth. Add the juice of 2 lemons, the tahini, 4 tablespoons of the cooking water, and salt to taste. Pulse once or twice and check the consistency. If necessary, add more

cooking water until the mixture forms a soft, creamy paste. It will thicken as it cools. Taste and adjust the seasoning. Transfer to a serving bowl, drizzle with olive oil, and sprinkle with the paprika. Set aside.

4 Peel the carrots and the cucumber. Trim the ends of the carrots and cut into sticks. Cut the cucumber in half lengthwise, scoop out the seeds, then cut into sticks. Trim the bunch of green onions, removing only the dark tops. Trim the radishes, leaving ¼ inch (6 mm) of the stem intact.

5 Preheat the broiler (grill). Arrange the carrots, cucumber, green onions, and radishes on a serving plate. Place the olives in a small bowl. Arrange the pita breads on a baking sheet and toast until hot and slightly crisp, 1–2 minutes per side.

6 Cut the pita breads into wedges and serve with the tabbouleh, hummus, vegetables, and olives.

Serve with a crisp Greek white wine from Santorini or an earthy red wine from Greece's Nemea region.

1 cup (6 oz/185 g) dried chickpeas (garbanzo beans), soaked overnight in water to cover

½ teaspoon baking soda (bicarbonate of soda)

⅔ cup (4 oz/125 g) bulgur wheat

3 green (spring) onions plus 1 bunch for serving

⅓ cup (3 fl oz/80 ml) extra-virgin olive oil plus more for drizzling

Juice of 3 lemons, or to taste

½ lb (125 g) tomatoes, peeled and finely chopped (see page 187)

2 cups (2 oz/60 g) flat-leaf (Italian) parsley leaves, finely chopped

Fine sea salt and pepper

1 clove garlic, crushed

3 tablespoons tahini

½ teaspoon paprika

3 carrots

1 small cucumber, about 6 inches (15 cm) long

1 bunch small radishes

1 cup whole, oil-cured green or black olives

6 pita breads

Makes 6 servings

SOUPS AND SALADS

A fresh seasonal salad and a cup of classic watercress soup can be the

oundation for an impromptu picnic lunch in one of London's many parks.

Soups and salads form an integral part of the London diet, served for lunch or dinner, as a starter or as a main course, depending on how hearty they are. In the summer, spicy crab salad with avocado and refreshing cucumber soup make use of fresh vegetables and seafood from London's farmers' markets. Spanish-inspired chickpea, chorizo, and roasted pepper salad is substantial enough for a light lunch, and arugula salad with quince cheese and thin slices of prosciutto stars on many smart restaurant menus. In the rainy winter months, nothing is more warming than a steaming bowl of pea soup.

CHICKPEA, TOMATO, AND CHORIZO SALAD

On Saturday mornings, London foodies head to Borough Market with its countless food stalls. The scent of chorizo sausages grilling over charcoal fills the air, and shoppers cannot resist eating a crusty sandwich filled with hot chorizo as they push through the crowds. The chorizo is sold by Brindisa, a small company that imports such Spanish delicacies as salted anchovies and paprika. Brindisa's products have transformed the city's menus, leading to widespread experimentation with Spanish ingredients, as in this salad.

1 To make the vinaigrette, in a large bowl, whisk together the olive oil, vinegar, and garlic. Season to taste with salt and black pepper. Set aside.

2 Preheat the broiler (grill). Place the red pepper quarters skin side up in a small roasting pan and broil (grill) until the skin blisters and blackens, about 5 minutes. Transfer to a small bowl and cover.

3 When the pepper quarters are cool enough to handle, peel off the skin. Cut the flesh into large dice. Add to the vinaigrette along with the tomatoes, onion, chickpeas, and parsley. Season to taste with cayenne, salt, and black pepper.

4 In a large frying pan over medium heat, warm the olive oil. Add the chorizo and fry until crisp, 2–3 minutes on each side. Transfer to paper towels to drain.

5 Add the chorizo to the salad and toss to combine. Taste and adjust the seasoning. Serve at once. The salad can be prepared up to 4 hours in advance and stored in the refrigerator. Bring to room temperature for 20 minutes, then garnish with parsley before serving.

Serve with a spicy, medium-bodied Spanish red wine such as Rioja Crianza.

FOR THE VINAIGRETTE

6 tablespoons (3 fl oz/90 ml) extra-virgin olive oil

2 tablespoons red wine vinegar

1 clove garlic, finely chopped

Fine sea salt and freshly ground black pepper

2 red bell peppers (capsicums), quartered and seeded

1 lb (500 g) tomatoes, peeled and diced (see page 187)

1 small red onion, diced

2 cans (15 oz/470 g each) sodium-free chickpeas (garbanzo beans), drained and rinsed

1 cup (1 oz/30 g) flat-leaf (Italian) parsley leaves, coarsely chopped, plus more for garnish

Pinch of cayenne pepper, or to taste

Fine sea salt and freshly ground black pepper

1 tablespoon olive oil

½ lb (250 g) Spanish chorizo sausage, cut into half moons

Makes 4 servings

Butchers

Every Saturday morning, a queue spills out from C. Lidgate, the butcher shop on Holland Park Avenue. Inside, butchers frantically work to fill customers' orders —weighing homemade sausages, cutting joints of Aberdeen Angus beef, and measuring chops of Gloucester Old Spot pork. During winter months, Lidgate sells plump geese and game such as grouse and pheasant, and even offers a plucking and hanging service for Londoners who have returned from a weekend shooting.

In recent years, London butchers have developed a fashionable niche market for organic meat and specific breeds purchased directly from farms. Lidgate, for example, buys organic beef and pork from Highgrove, Prince Charles's estate in Wiltshire. Some farmers have even opted to sell their meat directly to customers at London farmers' markets. The Ginger Pig, for example, was so successful in Borough Market selling meat from its Yorkshire farm that it opened a butcher shop in Marylebone. Customers can purchase Ginger Pig bacon, made from dapper Berkshire or long-flanked Tamworth pigs, or order meltingly tender Swaledale lamb, a hardy hill breed.

SPICY CRAB, AVOCADO, AND WATERCRESS SALAD

In the 1970s, nearly every London bistro served an avocado and crab or shrimp (prawn) cocktail. The seafood was bathed in a lightly spiced tomato mayonnaise and piled into an avocado half placed on a bed of lettuce. Chefs gradually started to experiment with this iconic dish, and today you can order a superb classic crab salad seasoned and plated at your table, as at Cecconi's in Mayfair. Or try the light, spicy version here, where the crab is dressed in a modest amount of mayonnaise and spiked with fresh lime juice, mint, and chiles. Rather than cook whole crabs, you can purchase freshly cooked lump crabmeat.

FOR THE CRAB SALAD

3 cups (18 oz/560 g) fresh lump crabmeat

1 or 2 red or green chiles such as Thai or serrano, finely diced

Finely grated zest of 2 limes

Juice of 1 lime

2 tablespoons coarsely chopped fresh mint

2 tablespoons mayonnaise

Fine sea salt

FOR THE DRESSING

6 tablespoons (3 fl oz/90 ml) extra-virgin olive oil

2 tablespoons fresh lime juice

Fine sea salt and freshly ground pepper

1 small red onion

2 hearts of romaine (cos) lettuce, leaves separated and torn into pieces

2 bunches watercress, trimmed into sprigs

3 avocados

Makes 6 servings

1 To make the crab salad, place the crabmeat in a medium bowl. Pick over the crabmeat to make sure that all pieces of shell have been removed. Using a paper towel, gently pat the crabmeat dry. Add the chiles, lime zest and juice, mint, and mayonnaise to the crabmeat. Stir gently to combine. Season to taste with salt, cover, and refrigerate until serving.

2 To make the dressing, in a small bowl, whisk together the olive oil and lime juice. Season to taste with salt and pepper.

3 Halve the onion lengthwise, peel, then slice thinly. Set aside one-fourth of it to use as garnish. In a large bowl, combine the onion, lettuce, and watercress. Drizzle with the dressing and toss gently to combine.

4 Halve each avocado and remove the pit. Peel each avocado half or, using a large metal spoon, carefully scoop the flesh of the avocado half from the peel in one piece. Discard the peel.

5 Divide the greens and onion among 6 individual plates. Top each with an avocado half. Spoon one-sixth of the crabmeat mixture onto each avocado half. Garnish with the remaining onion, and serve.

Serve with a rich white Burgundy such as Meursault or a Tuscan Chardonnay.

WATERCRESS SOUP

Bunches of watercress have been hawked on London's streets for centuries and eaten by residents as a cure-all for winter ailments. Only in the last seventy years have greengrocers and markets sold watercress, which remains a favorite salad ingredient. The peppery green leaves are popular in creamy soups that can be eaten hot or chilled, and restaurants ranging from the Michelin-starred Orrery to the casual No. 6 George Street serve it all summer. Hot watercress soup is often topped with crisp croutons, while cold soup is given a swirl of cream.

1 In a large saucepan over medium heat, warm the olive oil. Add the onion and cook, stirring occasionally, until soft, about 5 minutes. Stir in the potatoes and cook for 2 minutes. Add the leeks, raise the heat to medium-high, and cook, stirring occasionally, until the leeks begin to soften and wilt, about 4 minutes. Add the chicken stock and season with salt and pepper. Raise the heat to high, bring to a boil, then reduce the heat to medium-low, and simmer, uncovered, until the vegetables are very soft, about 25 minutes.

2 Strip the watercress leaves from the stems and discard the stems. Add the leaves to the saucepan and cook just until they are soft enough to purée, about 3 minutes. The longer the watercress leaves cook, the more their color will fade.

3 Purée the soup with an immersion blender or transfer to a food processor and purée. Stir in the cream. Taste and adjust the seasoning.

4 If serving the soup hot, gently reheat over medium heat. To serve the soup cold, transfer to a serving bowl, cover, and refrigerate for 4 hours or until chilled.

Serve with a lemony, crisp white wine such as Chablis.

¼ cup (2 fl oz/60 ml) olive oil

1 yellow onion, coarsely diced

2 large Yukon gold potatoes, peeled and diced

1 lb (500 g) leeks, white and pale green parts only, thinly sliced

4 cups (32 fl oz/1 l) homemade chicken stock or water

Fine sea salt and freshly ground pepper

2 bunches watercress

1 cup (8 fl oz/250 ml) heavy (double) cream

Makes 4 servings

English Asparagus

Beginning early in May, bundles of English asparagus are sold across the city. Street and market vendors bellow out offers of "two for the price of one" for bunches of pencil-thin sprue asparagus. Restaurants offer an array of exquisite dishes—puréed asparagus soup or simple salads with grilled spears. The season is brief, a mere six weeks, but it marks the beginning of summer for Londoners, who will find any excuse to eat a plateful of tender spears dipped in melted butter or vinaigrette. Naturally, they believe English asparagus is the finest in the world.

Farmers claim that the temperate British weather causes the plants to grow slowly, which allows them to develop a superb taste. Most of the London crop comes from the Fens, north of the city. In centuries past, asparagus was grown in kitchen gardens surrounding London and along the Thames estuary and was known as sparrow grass. In the seventeenth and eighteenth centuries, growers extended the season, and the price, by making composted hotbeds. Today, imported asparagus is available year-round, but none compares with the flavor of homegrown asparagus.

BELGIAN ENDIVE, PEAR, FETA, AND WALNUT SALAD

Londoners love good, simple food—especially food with a provenance. To ensure that a salad like this one tastes superb, they will seek out barrel-cured Greek feta cheese and French wet walnuts from specialty shops such as La Fromagerie, and the sweetest, ripest local organic pears, such as Comice or Concord, from their farmers' market. This trend began in the 1980s with London chefs Sally Clarke of & Clarke's and Rowley Leigh of Kensington Place, who listed on their menus some of their best sources of ingredients, whether a purveyor of greens or a seller of a particular breed of duck.

FOR THE VINAIGRETTE

6 tablespoons (3 fl oz/90 ml) walnut oil

2 tablespoons white wine vinegar or Champagne vinegar

Fine sea salt and freshly ground pepper

FOR THE SALAD

4 heads Belgian endive (chicory/witloof)

¼ cup (⅓ oz/10 g) coarsely snipped chives

1 cup (4 oz/125 g) walnut halves

½ lb (250 g) feta cheese, crumbled into ½-inch (12-cm) pieces

4 small ripe pears such as Comice or Concord

Makes 4 servings

1 To make the vinaigrette, in a small bowl, whisk together the walnut oil and vinegar. Season to taste with salt and pepper. Set aside.

2 To make the salad, separate the leaves of the endive. In a large bowl, combine the endive leaves, chives, walnuts, and feta cheese.

3 If desired, peel the pears. Cut each pear lengthwise into quarters and, using a small, sharp knife, remove the core from each pear. Cut each quarter lengthwise into thin slices.

4 Add the pear slices to the salad, drizzle with the vinaigrette, and toss gently to combine. Taste and adjust the seasoning. Divide the salad among 4 individual plates and serve at once.

Serve with a buttery white Burgundy such as Meursault or an apple-scented Bourgogne Blanc.

CHILLED CUCUMBER SOUP

A bowl of cool, fresh-tasting cucumber soup is perfect for a hot summer day in London and is often served in restaurants and at home. English cucumbers, a long, smooth-skinned variety, first became popular in London in the eighteenth century. They were grown under glass cloches in hotbeds in the thriving market gardens of Pimlico, Fulham, Chelsea, Kensington, and other surrounding rural villages, where farmers also specialized in rare and out-of-season fruits and vegetables such as melons and winter asparagus. This classic recipe is updated with crème fraîche.

1 In a small saucepan over low heat, combine the milk, onion, bay leaf, and peppercorns. Heat the milk mixture slowly until small bubbles form around the edge of the pan, about 5 minutes. Remove from the heat, cover, and let stand for 30 minutes to infuse the milk with the seasonings.

2 Peel the cucumbers. Halve each cucumber lengthwise and scoop out the seeds with a teaspoon. Set aside half of one cucumber for garnish. Cut the remaining 3½ cucumbers crosswise into thick slices. In a large saucepan over medium-low heat, melt the butter. Add the cucumber slices and sugar, season with salt and pepper, and cook until the cucumber is soft, stirring occasionally, 4–5 minutes. Stir in the flour and cook, stirring, until the butter and flour thicken, about 3 minutes. Stir in the chicken stock, bring to a boil, and cook until thickened slightly, about 5 minutes.

3 Strain the milk mixture through a fine-mesh sieve into the saucepan and stir thoroughly. Simmer uncovered over medium-low heat, stirring occasionally, until the soup has thickened, about 20 minutes.

4 Purée the soup with an immersion blender or transfer to a food processor and purée. Stir in the crème fraîche and season to taste with salt and pepper. Transfer to a bowl, cover, and refrigerate until chilled, about 4 hours.

5 To serve, finely dice the remaining cucumber half. Ladle the chilled soup into individual bowls and garnish with the diced cucumber and the dill.

Serve with a refreshing, very dry white wine such as Muscadet or Sancerre.

1¼ cups (10 fl oz/310 ml) whole milk

1 small yellow onion, halved

1 fresh or dried bay leaf

2 peppercorns

4 English (hothouse) cucumbers

2 tablespoons unsalted butter

Pinch of sugar

Fine sea salt and freshly ground pepper

2 tablespoons all-purpose (plain) flour

2 cups (16 fl oz/500 ml) home-made chicken stock

¾ cup (6 oz/185 g) crème fraîche

1 teaspoon finely chopped fresh dill

Makes 4 servings

SORREL, LETTUCE, AND QUAIL EGG SALAD

Leafy green salads are popular among Londoners throughout the summer months. Fresh herbs, such as sorrel, mint, chervil, or tarragon, are often mixed in with choice salad leaves from farmers' markets. The salads are transformed by adding seasonal ingredients such as blanched green beans, asparagus tips, or fava beans, with lightly cooked quail eggs or crisp bacon. Sorrel has a superb lemony acidity, which imbues the salad with a refreshing bite. Although sorrel is not easy to replicate, you can use another favorite salad leaf such as mizuna. Similarly, one of the above vegetables can be substituted for the quail eggs.

12 quail eggs

2 bunches sorrel leaves, about 4 oz (125 g) total weight

2 heads butter (Boston) lettuce

3 fresh tarragon sprigs

6 green (spring) onions, white parts only, thinly sliced

3 tablespoons extra-virgin olive oil

1 tablespoon tarragon vinegar

1 teaspoon Dijon mustard

Fine sea salt and freshly ground pepper

Makes 4 servings

1 In a small saucepan, combine the quail eggs with cold water to cover. Bring to a boil over high heat and boil for 2 minutes. Immediately plunge the eggs into cold water. Set aside to cool.

2 Strip away the stems of the sorrel leaves by folding the sides of each leaf inward and pulling the stem toward the tip of the leaf. This will split the leaf in half. Tear the halves into bite-sized pieces and place in a bowl. Remove the outer leaves from each head of butter lettuce until you reach the heart. Reserve the outer leaves for another use. Separate the leaves from each heart, rinse, and dry. Add to the bowl with the sorrel leaves and toss to combine. Strip the leaves from the tarragon stems and add to the salad with the sliced green onions.

3 Peel each quail egg under cold running water, being sure to remove every speck of eggshell. Pat the eggs dry with a kitchen towel. Cut the eggs in half and add to the salad.

4 In a small bowl, whisk together the olive oil, vinegar, mustard, and salt and pepper to taste. Drizzle over the salad and toss gently to combine.

5 Arrange the salad on individual plates, dividing the quail eggs evenly. Serve at once.

Serve with a smoky, dry white Sauvignon Blanc such as Pouilly-Fumé or Quincy.

ASIAN GRILLED SALMON SALAD

Over the past thirty years, Londoners have developed a taste for Asian cuisine, in particular, Japanese, Chinese, and Thai cooking. Initially, in the early 1980s, London cooks would haphazardly mix the different styles. A Japanese chicken teriyaki, for example, might be paired with Chinese pickled cucumbers. Gradually, as Londoners' culinary knowledge expanded, they developed a fusion of ingredients, flavors, and cooking techniques to create a new style of modern British cooking. This contemporary salad exemplifies these influences.

1 To make the marinade, in a small nonreactive saucepan, combine the soy sauce, honey, and ginger. Set over low heat and cook, stirring, until the honey is dissolved. Simmer for 1 minute and remove from the heat. Add the lime zest and let stand to cool to room temperature and to infuse the honey mixture, about 30 minutes. Whisk in the lime juice and sesame oil. Set aside.

2 In a bowl, combine the cucumber and ¼ teaspoon salt and let stand for 10 minutes. Stir in the sugar and vinegar. In a large bowl, combine the lettuce, arugula, and green onions. Set aside.

3 Run your fingers gently over each salmon fillet to locate the pin bones and remove them with sturdy tweezers or needle-nosed pliers. In a nonstick frying pan over high heat, warm the olive oil. Add the fillets skin side down and cook until crisp, about 5 minutes. Turn and cook until golden, 5 minutes longer. Transfer to a dish and generously spoon half of the marinade over the fillets. Let stand until cool.

4 Before serving, remove the skin from each fillet and discard the skin. Add the remaining marinade and the cucumber and any liquid to the salad and toss to combine. Divide the salad among individual plates. Top each salad with a salmon fillet and serve at once.

Serve with Pilsner beer or a dry white wine such as Alsatian Riesling.

FOR THE MARINADE

¼ cup (2 fl oz/60 ml) naturally brewed soy sauce (see page 187)

3 tablespoons honey

1 tablespoon peeled and finely grated fresh ginger

Finely grated zest of 2 limes

Juice of I lime

1 tablespoon Asian sesame oil

1 garden (ridge) cucumber, peeled and finely sliced

Fine sea salt

1 tablespoon sugar

1 tablespoon white wine vinegar

4 heads Bibb lettuce, leaves separated

1 bunch (1 oz/30 g) arugula (rocket), trimmed

6 green (spring) onions, white parts only, thinly sliced

4 salmon fillets, about 6 oz (185 g) each

3 tablespoons olive oil

Makes 4 servings

Asian Shops

Despite London's vast size, the city is made up of villagelike communities whose character is shaped in part by the different nationalities living there. With each influx of immigrants come new foods, shops, and restaurants. The Japanese, for example, have settled north of the center of London along Finchley Road, where small shops have shelves stacked with mirin, bonito flakes, and dried seaweed and counters filled with glistening fresh fish.

Thai shops are scattered throughout London, but Richmond has particularly good ones, including Paya Thai and Talad Thai. Here, cooks can buy tiny pea eggplants (aubergines), holy basil, fresh galangal, and myriad spices and dry goods for flavoring curries and soups. Peckham and Dalston are known for Vietnamese stores, while Earl's Court has a Filipino shop selling a wide range of foods from purple yam jam to fresh banana leaves.

Most Londoners seeking exotic Chinese ingredients head for Chinatown in Soho, where well-stocked shops carry spices, dried mushrooms, wonton wrappers, Burmese pickles, and fresh lotus roots.

ARUGULA SALAD WITH QUINCE CHEESE AND PROSCIUTTO

Every autumn, fragrant golden quinces are piled high in London's Middle Eastern food shops. Discerning customers bring them home to prepare syrups, puddings, and, best of all, quince cheese. Known also by its Spanish name, membrillo, *quince cheese has been made in England since the sixteenth century, when fruit pastes were served at the end of a meal with nuts and other sweetmeats. The cheese is enjoying renewed popularity with chefs such as Henry Harris of Racine and Samuel and Samantha Clark of Moro, who use it in starters such as this one, where it balances the salty prosciutto and peppery arugula.*

FOR THE QUINCE CHEESE

3 lb (1.5 kg) quinces

Juice of 2 lemons

1½–2 lb (750 g–1 kg) sugar, or as needed

1½ teaspoons sunflower oil

FOR THE SALAD

1 teaspoon fresh lemon juice

1½ tablespoons extra-virgin olive oil

Fine sea salt and freshly ground pepper

5 oz (155 g) arugula (rocket), trimmed

9 oz (280 g) thinly sliced prosciutto

Makes 6 servings

1 To make the quince cheese, scrub the quinces well and then coarsely chop without peeling or coring them. Place in a large nonreactive saucepan with the lemon juice and enough water just to cover. Bring to a boil over high heat, reduce the heat to low, cover, and simmer until the quinces are very soft and a deep brownish pink, about 3 hours.

2 Pass the quince mixture through a fine-mesh sieve set over a bowl, pressing on the solids with the back of a wooden spoon to extract as much purée as possible. Discard the solids. Measure the purée and allow 1 lb (500 g) sugar for every 2 cups (18 oz/560 g) of purée. Combine the purée and sugar in a large nonreactive saucepan, place over low heat, and cook, stirring, until the sugar is dissolved. Raise the heat to high, bring to a boil, and continue to cook, stirring constantly, until the mixture is so thick that the spoon leaves a clean line when drawn across the pan bottom and the purée is a uniformly dark, dusky pink, about 25 minutes. As the hot purée thickens, it will splatter, so protect your arms by wearing oven mitts and/or long sleeves.

3 Meanwhile, to sterilize jars for storing the quince cheese for up to 1 year, preheat the oven to 125°F (52°C). Wash three 1-cup (8–fl oz/250-ml) wide-mouth glass jam jars in warm soapy water, rinse in clean warm water, and set in the oven to dry. Lightly oil the sterilized jars with the sunflower oil, then spoon the hot quince mixture into the jars to within ¼ inch (6 mm) of the tops. Wipe the rims clean with a hot, damp kitchen towel, top with metal canning lids, and seal tightly with screw bands. Process in a boiling-water bath for 15 minutes. Using tongs, transfer the jars to a kitchen towel and let cool. Store in a cool, dark place. The quince cheese will keep for up to 1 year.

4 Alternatively, to set and store the quince cheese for up to 1 month, lightly oil three sterilized 1-cup (8–fl oz/250-ml) ramekins. Spoon the hot quince mixture into the ramekins to within ¼ inch (6 mm) of the tops. Let the mixture cool, cover tightly with plastic wrap, and store in the refrigerator for up to 1 month.

5 Turn out the quince cheese from one of the jars or ramekins. Dip a sharp knife into very hot water and cut the cheese into slices ¼ inch (6 mm) thick. Then trim the slices into triangles or diamonds. Set the slices aside.

6 To make the salad, in a large bowl, whisk together the lemon juice, olive oil, and salt and pepper to taste. Add the arugula and toss thoroughly. Arrange the prosciutto on 6 individual plates. Divide the arugula salad among the plates and scatter with the quince cheese triangles. Serve at once.

Serve with a creamy sherry from Spain such as Oloroso.

PEA SOUP

In the nineteenth century, soup made from dried peas was sold from street barrows around London to those keen for a quick, hot dinner. The peas were cooked into a very thick soup that not only was filling but also helped fend off the damp winter chill. The soup was known as London Particular after the famously dense, sulfurous smog that enveloped the city. To this day, very thick fog is called a pea souper. Old-fashioned winter pea soups such as this recipe are made with split peas, while lighter versions use English peas. The former tend to be served in pubs or brasseries specializing in hearty fare.

1 Place the peas in a large bowl, add cold water to cover generously, and let soak for at least 12 hours or up to overnight.

2 The next day, in a large saucepan over low heat, warm the sunflower oil. Add the bacon and cook, stirring frequently, until it releases its fat, about 3 minutes. Add the onion, garlic, carrot, and celery and cook, stirring occasionally, until soft, about 10 minutes.

3 Drain the peas and add to the pan along with the parsley leaves and 7 cups (56 fl oz/1.75 l) water. Bring to a boil over high heat, reduce the heat to low, cover partially, and simmer until the peas are meltingly soft, about 2 hours. Halfway through the cooking time, add about 2½ cups (20 fl oz/625 ml) water to replenish the cooking liquid.

4 Purée the soup with an immersion blender or transfer to a food processor and purée. Strain the puréed soup through a coarse-mesh sieve into a clean saucepan. Gently reheat over medium-low heat, stirring occasionally and diluting the soup with water if it is too thick. Season to taste with salt and pepper.

5 Ladle the soup into warmed bowls, garnish with the parsley leaves if desired, and serve at once.

Serve with a smoky white wine such as Pinot Gris.

1 cup (7 oz/220 g) yellow or green split peas, picked over, rinsed, and drained

2 tablespoons sunflower oil

¼ lb (125 g) bacon, finely diced

1 yellow onion, coarsely diced

1 clove garlic, coarsely chopped

1 carrot, peeled and coarsely diced

2 celery stalks, coarsely diced

Leaves of 1 fresh flat-leaf (Italian) parsley sprig, plus more for garnish (optional)

Fine sea salt and freshly ground pepper

Makes 4 servings

MAIN COURSES

From savory pies to classic roasts, contemporary seasonal dishes to kebabs and

curries, main dishes are defined by the delicious diversity of London cuisine.

Main dishes are characterized by their ability to stand alone as the well-balanced course of a meal. Hearty fish pie topped with mashed potatoes, succulent roast beef with Yorkshire pudding, and steak, mushroom, and ale pie reflect an attachment to beloved traditions. The city's international character is evident in the long-standing popularity of Chinese, Indian, and Middle Eastern cuisines. As in other culinary meccas, chefs cook with the seasons, preparing lamb in spring and pheasant in autumn. Bacon and egg butties and bangers and mash fill the need for food that is both quick and satisfying.

FISH AND CHIPS

Londoners are fond of "going round to the chippie" to fetch piping-hot fried fish and salted deep-fried potatoes. The chips are further seasoned with malt vinegar before being enclosed with the fish in paper. The wrapping was once newspaper, but it was banned years ago, despite claims that the printer's ink added a special flavor. The origin of fish and chips is uncertain. The selling of fried fish on London streets appeared in Charles Dickens's 1837 novel Oliver Twist, and by the 1850s, fried fish and cooked "shaved" potatoes were hawked on city streets. In 1860, Joseph Malin opened the first known fish-and-chip shop.

1 To make the chips, cut the potatoes lengthwise into sticks about ¼ inch (6 mm) thick. Place in a bowl of cold water and set aside to soak for 20 minutes to remove the excess starch.

2 While the potatoes are soaking, begin to prepare the fish: Spread the flour on a plate and season with salt and pepper. Place the bread crumbs on a separate plate. Crack the egg into a shallow bowl, beat lightly, and season with salt and pepper. Dust each fish fillet with the seasoned flour, then dip into the beaten egg, letting the excess drip back into the bowl. Finally, dredge in the bread crumbs, lightly pressing the crumbs onto all sides. Place the coated fillets in a single layer on a plate. Lightly cover with plastic wrap and refrigerate until you are ready to cook the fish.

3 In a large, heavy frying pan over medium-high heat, pour in enough sunflower oil to reach a depth of 4 inches (10 cm). Heat to 325°F (165°C) on a deep-frying thermometer. Drain the potato sticks and pat dry with paper towels or a clean kitchen towel. Working in batches, carefully place the potato sticks in the hot oil and fry until crisp but not browned on the outside and tender but slightly firm on the inside, about 4 minutes. Do not overcrowd the pan or the oil will not be able to maintain the proper temperature. Using a slotted spoon, lift the potatoes from the hot oil,

letting it drip back into the pan, and transfer to a wire rack lined with paper towels to drain. When the oil returns to 325°F (165°C), fry the remaining potatoes. When the potatoes have cooled, they can be laid on a baking sheet lined with paper towels and refrigerated for up to 4 hours until needed. Allow to return to room temp-erature before the second frying.

4 Shortly before you are ready to serve the chips, reheat the oil to 350°F (180°C). Again working in batches, carefully place the potatoes in the hot oil and cook until golden and crisp, 4–5 minutes. Transfer to paper towels to drain. Sprinkle with salt and toss gently.

5 To cook the fish, pour in enough oil to generously cover the bottom of a large nonstick frying pan and set over medium heat. When the oil is hot, add the coated fillets and cook until golden brown, about 4 minutes. Turn and cook until golden brown on the second side, 4–6 minutes. The timing will depend on the thickness of the fillets; do not let the bread crumbs burn. Transfer the fillets to paper towels to drain.

6 Divide the fish and chips among 4 warmed individual plates. Garnish with the parsley sprigs and lemon quarters and serve at once.

Serve with a pint of pale ale or a full-bodied Chardonnay.

FOR THE CHIPS

4 large russet potatoes, peeled

Sunflower or corn oil for deep-frying

Fine sea salt

FOR THE FISH

2 tablespoons all-purpose (plain) flour

Fine sea salt and freshly ground pepper

2 cups (8 oz/250 g) dried white bread crumbs

1 large egg

4 cod or haddock fillets, about 5 oz (155 g) each, skin removed

Sunflower oil for panfrying

4 fresh flat-leaf (Italian) parsley sprigs

1 lemon, quartered

Makes 4 servings

BANGERS AND MASH WITH RED ONION AND WINE GRAVY

Sausages roasted until mahogany brown and served with mashed potatoes and a rich onion gravy are a favorite dish at local pubs and cafés, and even at Michelin-starred restaurants. The British sausage became known as a banger around World War I, probably because it spluttered as it fried. The sausages traditionally contain bread crumbs mixed with minced pork, beef, or both. The bread gives them a softer consistency and a milder flavor than their continental counterparts. There are hundreds of recipes—often well-guarded secrets—the most famous being an unlinked spicy pork variety known as a Cumberland.

2 lb (1 kg) good-quality pork sausages

1 tablespoon sunflower oil

FOR THE MASH

2 lb (1 kg) Yukon gold potatoes, peeled and cut into large chunks

Fine sea salt and freshly ground pepper

⅓ cup (3 fl oz/80 ml) whole milk

2 tablespoons unsalted butter

FOR THE GRAVY

2 tablespoons unsalted butter

1 tablespoon olive oil

2 red onions, halved and finely sliced

1½ teaspoons all-purpose (plain) flour

1 teaspoon red wine vinegar

1 cup (8 fl oz/250 ml) red wine, such as Shiraz

1 cup (8 fl oz/250 ml) homemade chicken or beef stock

Fine sea salt and freshly ground pepper

Makes 4 servings

1 Preheat the oven to 400°F (200°C). Place the sausages in a roasting pan, drizzle with the oil, toss to coat, and spread out in a single layer. Bake, turning them after 15 minutes, until evenly colored, about 30 minutes.

2 Meanwhile, to make the mash, place the potato chunks in a saucepan with water to cover, salt the water, and bring to a boil over medium heat. This will take about 15 minutes. Continue to cook until the potatoes are tender when pierced with the tip of a knife, about 15 minutes longer. Drain in a colander, cover with a kitchen towel, and let stand until dry, about 5 minutes. In the same pan, combine the milk and butter, and bring to a boil over medium-high heat. Remove from the heat and set aside. For the fluffiest texture, pass the cooked potatoes through a food mill fitted with the medium disk or through a ricer. Alternatively, place in a bowl and mash with a potato masher. Pour in the hot milk mixture and beat until smooth. Season to taste with salt and pepper.

3 To make the gravy, in a wide, shallow nonreactive saucepan over medium-low heat, melt the butter with the olive oil. Add the onions and cook, stirring frequently, until collapsed, about 4 minutes. Reduce the heat to low, cover the onions with roughly crumpled parchment (baking) paper, pressing it down on the onions, and cook until the onions are meltingly soft, about 20 minutes. Remove the paper and raise the heat to medium-low. Using a wooden spoon, stir in the flour and cook until lightly colored, 2–3 minutes. Stir in the vinegar and cook until evaporated. Stir in the red wine and stock, raise the heat to medium, bring to a boil, and simmer until a luscious sauce forms, about 10 minutes. Season to taste with salt and pepper.

4 Divide the sausages and mash among warmed individual plates. Spoon some gravy over the sausages and serve at once. Pass the gravy at the table for guests.

Serve with a full-bodied amber beer, a Shiraz, or a red Beaujolais cru, such as Julienas or Morgon.

VENISON WITH RED WINE JUS AND ROASTED PARSNIPS

The arrival of autumn brings a change of emphasis in London restaurants. Gone from menus are summery fish dishes, replaced by heartier fare like venison with red wine jus, usually accompanied by root vegetables such as parsnips, celery root (celeriac), or beets. Chefs can buy wild or farmed roe, fallow, or red deer. Most prefer the tender, mild farmed deer, which is available year-round. The British traditionally eat venison with sweet-and-sour sauces such as red currant jelly or pears poached in red wine with peppercorns.

1 To make the jus, in a nonreactive saucepan over high heat, combine the shallot and wine, bring to a boil, and cook until reduced to about ¼ cup (2 fl oz/ 60 ml), about 20 minutes. Add the stock, bring to a boil, and cook until reduced to about ⅔ cup (5 fl oz/ 160 ml), about 40 minutes. Stir in the Port, reduce the heat to low, and quickly whisk in a few pieces of the diced butter, taking care not to let it boil. Whisk in the remaining butter, a few pieces at a time. Set aside.

2 To make the roasted parsnips, position a rack in the center of the oven and preheat to 350°F (180°C). Place the parsnips on a rimmed baking sheet large enough to arrange them in a single layer. Drizzle with the olive oil and toss to coat thoroughly. Season lightly with salt and pepper. Bake, stirring occasionally, until soft and golden, about 40 minutes.

3 Meanwhile, in a nonstick frying pan over high heat, warm the sunflower oil. When it is sizzling hot, season the venison steaks with salt and pepper, place in the pan, and cook until nicely browned, about 3 minutes. Turn and cook until a thermometer inserted into the center of a steak registers 125°–130°F (52°–54°C) for medium-rare, about 2 minutes.

4 Divide the steaks among individual plates. Spoon some red wine jus over the steaks, top each with the roasted parsnips, and serve at once.

Serve with a deep, red wine such as Bandol or a sturdy, full-bodied Cahors.

FOR THE RED WINE JUS

1 shallot, finely chopped

2 cups (16 fl oz/500 ml) dry red wine

4 cups (32 fl oz/1 l) homemade chicken stock

3 tablespoons Port

4 tablespoons (2 oz/60 g) cold unsalted butter, diced

FOR THE ROASTED PARSNIPS

1 lb (500 g) parsnips, trimmed, peeled, and cut lengthwise into quarters

3 tablespoons olive oil

Fine sea salt and freshly ground pepper

3 tablespoons sunflower oil

4 venison steaks, about 7 oz (220 g) each and ½ inch (12 mm) thick, trimmed of excess fat

Fine sea salt and freshly ground pepper

Makes 4 servings

Wine Merchants

Wine merchants have existed in London since Roman times. Over the centuries, they have stocked their cellars with fine English, French, German, Hungarian, Spanish, Italian, and New World wines. Compelled to buy wines that fit the nation's changing trade policies, merchants developed an extraordinary breadth of knowledge that has held them in good stead.

One example is Berry Bros. & Rudd on St. James's Street, the oldest wine shop in the city. With its shop front dating to the 1730s and its sloping floors, Berry Bros. & Rudd might seem at first glance like an old-fashioned wine merchant. It is, however, at the cutting edge of wine retailing. Behind the desks are computer screens, as much of the business comes from the company's innovative website. The staff are as adept at advising clients about building their cellar collection as they are in recommending a wine for dinner. The two-story cellar houses a selection from the shop's stock of 2,500 wines along with racks of dusty bottles, including such gems as a bottle of 1858 Lafite Rothschild claret owned by the Berry and Rudd families.

SEARED DUCK BREASTS WITH POMEGRANATE MOLASSES AND SPINACH

In 1997, Samuel and Samantha Clark opened Moro, a popular restaurant in Exmouth Market, where they developed a style that married Spanish, North African, and Middle Eastern influences with contemporary European cuisine. It was a culinary style that has since influenced many neighborhood restaurants. This recipe, adapted from a dish served at Moro, uses sweet-and-sour pomegranate molasses to add an intriguing undercurrent of flavor to cinnamon-spiced duck breasts. Pomegranate molasses, widely used in Middle Eastern cooking, has no ready substitute, but may be replaced with slightly sweetened tamarind syrup.

4 skin-on, boneless duck breasts, about 6 oz (185 g) each

⅛ teaspoon ground cinnamon

Fine sea salt and freshly ground pepper

1 small clove garlic, finely chopped

3 tablespoons pomegranate molasses

1 teaspoon honey (optional)

FOR THE SPINACH

1 tablespoon olive oil

4 green (spring) onions, white and pale green parts only, thinly sliced

1 lb (500 g) baby spinach leaves, washed, dried, and stems removed

Fine sea salt and freshly ground pepper

Makes 4 servings

1 Trim any sinews from the duck breasts. Using a sharp knife, score the skin in a crosshatch pattern, taking care not to cut into the meat. In a small bowl, stir together the cinnamon, 1 teaspoon salt, and a grinding of pepper. Rub the seasonings onto the duck breasts, especially on the skin. Place the duck breasts on a plate, cover with plastic wrap, and refrigerate for 2 hours.

2 Preheat the oven to 175°F (80°C). Select an ovenproof dish large enough to hold the duck breasts in a single layer and place it in the oven.

3 Set a frying pan over low heat and place the duck breasts in the pan, skin side down. Cook until the fat begins to render, about 3 minutes. Raise the heat to medium and cook until crisp and golden, about 5 minutes. Turn and cook until the meat is firm but still pinkish red when cut into with a sharp knife, about 5 minutes longer. Transfer the duck breasts to the warmed dish in the oven.

4 Pour off all but 1 tablespoon of the fat from the pan. Add the garlic and stir off the heat for about 45 seconds. When the pan has cooled slightly, place it over low heat, stir in the pomegranate molasses and 6 tablespoons (3 fl oz/90 ml) water, and cook until reduced slightly, about 1 minute. Season to taste with salt and pepper. The molasses is tart, so if you prefer a sweeter sauce, stir in the honey. Set the sauce aside.

5 To cook the spinach, in a wide saucepan over high heat, warm the olive oil. Add the green onions and cook, stirring occasionally, until softened, 2–3 minutes. Add the spinach to the pan, one handful at a time, and stir until wilted. When all the spinach is wilted, season to taste with salt and pepper.

6 To serve, reheat the sauce over medium heat. Slice each duck breast at an angle into 3 or 4 pieces and place on warmed individual plates. Add any accumulated juices in the dish to the sauce, raise the heat to high, bring to a boil, and pour over the breasts, dividing evenly. Spoon the spinach alongside the duck and serve at once.

Serve with a fruity red wine such as an Italian Primitivo or a smoky Syrah.

PANFRIED PHEASANT BREASTS WITH WILD MUSHROOM SAUCE

The Glorious Twelfth, the twelfth of August, marks the beginning of the game season, and in London, restaurants race to serve the first grouse of the season. On October 1, the game season begins in earnest with the arrival of plump little partridges and young pheasants. They are so popular that supermarkets now sell them whole and portioned into boneless breasts. In restaurants, pheasant breasts are often roasted and served either with a traditional bread sauce or a wild mushroom sauce like the one here. Accompany these panfried breasts with a creamy potato and celery root (celeriac) purée.

1 To make the marinade, in a nonreactive bowl, stir together 3 tablespoons of the olive oil, the lemon zest and juice, shallot, parsley sprigs, and a pinch of pepper. Wipe the pheasant breasts with damp kitchen towels and pick off any tiny feathers. Pat dry with paper towels. Place in the bowl with the marinade, turn to coat, cover with plastic wrap, and refrigerate for at least 1 hour or up to 3 hours.

2 To make the sauce, thickly slice or halve the mushrooms if they are large. In a wide saucepan over low heat, warm 2 tablespoons of the olive oil. Add the shallots and garlic and cook until soft, about 3 minutes. Raise the heat to medium, add the mushrooms, season to taste with salt and pepper, and cook until the mushrooms have softened slightly, about 3 minutes. Pour in the vermouth and boil until reduced to a few tablespoons, about 5 minutes. Add the chicken stock, chopped parsley, and thyme and

boil until the liquid has reduced by half, about 5 minutes. Swirl in the butter. Taste and adjust the seasoning. Keep the mushroom sauce warm over very low heat while you prepare the pheasant breasts.

3 To prepare the pheasant breasts, in a wide frying pan over medium-high heat, warm the remaining 3 tablespoons olive oil. Remove the pheasant breasts from the marinade, pat dry, and season lightly with salt. Place in the pan and cook until golden, about 2 minutes. Turn and cook just until the juices run clear when cut into with a sharp knife, 2–3 minutes longer. Do not overcook the meat or it will become tough.

4 Divide the pheasant breasts among warmed individual plates. Spoon on the mushroom sauce, dividing it evenly, and serve at once.

Serve with a rich, full-bodied aged red Burgundy or Châteauneuf-du-Pape.

8 tablespoons (4 fl oz/125 ml) olive oil

Finely grated zest of 1 lemon

2 tablespoons fresh lemon juice

1 shallot, thinly sliced

2 fresh flat-leaf (Italian) parsley sprigs, bruised

Freshly ground pepper

4 skinless, boneless pheasant breasts, about 5 oz (155 g) each

10 oz (315 g) wild mushrooms such as chanterelles and cepes, brushed clean and trimmed

2 shallots, finely chopped

1 clove garlic, finely chopped

Fine sea salt

½ cup (4 fl oz/125 ml) dry vermouth, such as Chamberry, or dry white wine

1 cup (8 fl oz/250 ml) homemade chicken stock

¼ cup (⅓ oz/10 g) chopped fresh flat-leaf (Italian) parsley

1 teaspoon chopped fresh thyme

2 tablespoons unsalted butter, diced

Makes 4 servings

STEAK, MUSHROOM, AND ALE PIE

Pies and pubs go together. Good gastropubs, pubs that specialize in both food and drink, serve satisfying savory pies, such as beef and mushroom or chicken and leek, often accompanied by potatoes and vegetables. Londoners have eaten pies since medieval times, when few houses had ovens. Consequently, many went to cookshops, or public eating houses, that sold pies and roasted meats as well as ale and wine. This tradition continues today, although many cooks bake pies at home. Rather than make your own puff pastry, you can purchase 1½ lb (750 g) of good-quality pastry from some bakeries and markets.

2 cups (10 oz/315 g) all-purpose (plain) flour, plus 5 tablespoons

Fine sea salt and ground pepper

1¼ cups (10 oz/315 g) cold unsalted butter

½ cup (4 fl oz/125 ml) cold water

3 sprigs *each* fresh flat-leaf (Italian) parsley and fresh thyme

2 whole cloves

1 bay leaf

6 tablespoons (3 fl oz/90 ml) sunflower oil, or as needed

2 lb (1 kg) beef rump roast, trimmed of fat and cut into 1-inch (2.5-cm) cubes

2 *each* yellow onions and large carrots, peeled and sliced, and celery stalks, thinly sliced

1 clove garlic, finely diced

½ lb (250 g) cremini mushrooms, brushed clean and trimmed

2 teaspoons brown sugar

2 tablespoons white wine vinegar

1 cup (8 fl oz/250 ml) light ale such as Stella Artois

3 strips lemon zest

1 egg, beaten

Makes 6 servings

1 To make the pastry, sift the 2 cups flour and a pinch of salt into a bowl. Finely dice 2 tablespoons of the butter. Using your fingertips, rub the butter into the flour until the mixture forms fine crumbs. Stir in the water to form a smooth dough. Turn the dough out onto a lightly floured work surface and knead until smooth. Flatten the dough, shape into a rectangle, wrap in plastic wrap, and refrigerate for at least 30 minutes.

2 Using a rolling pin, flatten the remaining butter into a rectangle ½ inch (12 mm) thick. On a lightly floured surface, roll the dough into a rectangle 3 times longer and 1 inch (2.5 cm) wider than the butter. Place the butter in the center of the dough and fold the dough over the butter so it is covered. Using the rolling pin, press down on the edges to seal. Turn the dough over and, with a short side facing you, roll out the dough until it returns to its original length. Fold the bottom third of the dough up and the top third down, as if folding a letter, then rotate the dough a quarter turn clockwise so that a fold is on your left (this is the first turn). Wrap the dough in plastic wrap and refrigerate for 30 minutes. Repeat to make 5 more turns, rotating the dough clockwise each time. If the dough becomes warm, refrigerate before continuing. When completed, wrap the dough in plastic wrap and refrigerate 1 hour.

3 Place the parsley and thyme sprigs, cloves, and bay leaf on a square of cheesecloth (muslin) and tie with kitchen string. Set aside. In a saucepan over medium heat, warm 3 tablespoons of the oil. Place 3 tablespoons of the flour on a plate and season with salt and pepper. Coat half of the beef cubes with the flour, shaking off the excess, and add to the pan in one layer. Brown the cubes on all sides, 4–6 minutes, transfer to a bowl, then repeat with the remaining beef cubes. Add the remaining oil to the pan, reduce the heat to low, add the onions, carrots, celery, and garlic, and cook, stirring occasionally, until soft, 8–10 minutes.

4 Raise the heat to medium, stir in the mushrooms and brown sugar, and cook until lightly browned, 2–3 minutes. Stir in the remaining 2 tablespoons flour and cook for 3–4 minutes. Add the vinegar, cook for 30 seconds, then add the ale, lemon zest strips, cheesecloth bundle, 1¼ cups (10 fl oz/310 ml) water, and the beef. Stir, bring to a boil, reduce the heat to low, cover, and simmer until the meat is tender, 1½ hours. Taste and adjust the seasoning. Set aside to cool for 1 hour.

5 Line a baking sheet with parchment (baking) paper. Have ready six 1½-cup (12–fl oz/375-ml) baking dishes. On a floured work surface, roll out the pastry into a rectangle ¼ inch (6 mm) thick. Cut the pastry into 6 rounds that are ¼ inch larger than the top of the baking dishes. Arrange on the baking sheet, prick the surface with a fork, and refrigerate for 30 minutes.

6 Preheat the oven to 400°F (200°C). Remove the cheesecloth bundle and lemon zest. Divide the filling among the 6 baking dishes. Brush the rim of each dish with the beaten egg. Lay a pastry round on top and press the edges down with a fork. Brush the top with beaten egg. Bake the pies for 15 minutes. Reduce the oven temperature to 350°F (180°C) and bake until golden brown, about 25 minutes longer. Serve at once.

BACON AND EGG BUTTIES

Bacon and eggs have been regarded by the British as wholesome fare since the sixteenth century but were put into sandwiches only in the latter part of the nineteenth century, when sandwiches became popular. Londoners, always keen on slang, refer to their bacon sandwiches as "bacon sarnies" or "bacon butties." The best are made at home, but they can be bought from neighborhood corner cafés or sandwich bars throughout the city. Regarded as the perfect pick-me-up, they are enjoyed anytime of day.

1 If using rolls, slice them in half. Generously butter the rolls or bread slices and divide among 4 plates. Set aside.

2 Set 2 large frying pans over medium-high heat and add 2 tablespoons sunflower oil to each pan. When the oil is sizzling hot, add half of the bacon in a single layer to each pan and cook until the bacon begins to color and become crisp, 2 minutes. Turn and cook until crisp on the second side, 2 minutes.

3 Stack the bacon slices in each pan and push to one side. Reduce the heat to low and gently crack 2 eggs into each pan without breaking the yolks. Cook the eggs for 1 minute. Turn and cook until the yolk is partially set but still somewhat soft, 1–2 minutes, or until done to your taste.

4 Divide the bacon slices among the plates, placing them on one of the buttered bread slices. Top with a fried egg and season to taste with salt and pepper. Cover with the remaining bread slices, buttered side down, and press firmly. Cut the sandwiches in half and serve at once.

Serve with tea, coffee, or chilled Champagne.

**4 good-quality soft white rolls or
8 thick slices cottage loaf or
good-quality white bread**

Softened unsalted butter as needed

**4 tablespoons (2 fl oz/60 ml)
sunflower oil**

**1 lb (500 g) applewood-smoked
or other good-quality bacon**

4 large free-range or organic eggs

**Fine sea salt and freshly
ground pepper**

Makes 4 servings

London's Classic Cafés

Fifty years ago, a new form of café arrived in cosmopolitan Soho. In 1953, Gina Lollabrigida opened Moka on Frith Street, which served as a template for the hundreds of London cafés that followed. These new cafés, also called coffee bars and later affectionately known as greasy spoons, were dominated by a steaming espresso machine, the recent invention of Achille Gaggia.

The cafés were at the cutting edge of postwar culture and became hotbeds of creativity for the film, fashion, music, literary, and advertising worlds. Each café attracted a different crowd, but perhaps the most famous was 2i's in Soho, a cellar frequented by musicians including the Beatles and Little Richard. By 1960, London had five hundred cafés, where young people hung out, drinking cappuccino and eating fry-ups of eggs, sausages, bacon, tomatoes, baked beans, and bread. Moka and 2i's are long gone, but newer classics, such as E. Pellicci on Bethnel Green Road and Bar Italia on Frith Street, now fill the void. London cafés remain places where all classes of society sit side by side as they savor a croissant or read the paper.

ROAST BEEF AND YORKSHIRE PUDDING

On Sunday mornings, the enticing aroma of roasting beef wafts down London streets. It conjures up the tempting taste of everyone's favorite Sunday dinner: roast beef and Yorkshire pudding, the latter a batter baked in the hot drippings from the beef. First appearing in the eighteenth century, the dish is believed to have originated in the north of England. It is still a treat to eat roast beef at such venerable London establishments as Simpson's-in-the-Strand, favored by Charles Dickens and William Gladstone, or the Grill Room in the Dorchester Hotel, patronized by Winston Churchill, Peter Sellers, and Elizabeth Taylor.

2-rib standing rib roast, about 4½ lb (2.25 kg)

1 tablespoon sunflower oil

Fine sea salt and freshly ground pepper

FOR THE YORKSHIRE PUDDING

1 cup (5 oz/155 g) all-purpose (plain) flour

¼ teaspoon fine sea salt

2 large eggs, beaten

¾ cup (6 fl oz/180 ml) whole milk

FOR THE HORSERADISH SAUCE

3 tablespoons freshly grated horseradish

¾ cup (6 oz/185 g) crème fraîche

Fine sea salt and freshly ground pepper

FOR THE GRAVY

2 tablespoons all-purpose (plain) flour

½ cup (4 fl oz/125 ml) dry white wine

1¾ cups (14 fl oz/430 ml) homemade beef stock

Makes 6 servings

1 Preheat the oven to 325°F (165°C). Place a rack in a roasting pan just large enough to hold the roast. Rub the meat all over with the sunflower oil and season with salt and pepper. Place fat side up on the rack and roast until an instant-read thermometer inserted into the thickest part away from the bone registers 125°–130°F (52°–54°C) for medium-rare, about 1 hour and 40 minutes.

2 Meanwhile, to make the Yorkshire pudding, sift the flour and salt into a bowl. Make a well in the center and gradually add the eggs, beating with a wooden spoon until smooth. Add ¼ cup (2 fl oz/ 60 ml) of the milk and beat until a thick, smooth batter forms. Gradually beat in the remaining milk and then beat vigorously for 1 minute longer. Cover the bowl with plastic wrap and set aside for 1 hour.

3 To make the horseradish sauce, in a small bowl, stir together the horseradish, crème fraîche, and salt and pepper to taste. Set aside.

4 When the roast is done, remove it from the oven. Transfer to a platter, tent loosely with aluminum foil, and set aside in a warm place. Raise the oven temperature to 425°F (220°C). Place six 1-cup (8–fl oz/ 250-ml) popover or muffin molds on a baking sheet. Spoon ½ teaspoon of the beef drippings from the roasting pan into each of the molds. Place in the oven until the fat is sizzling hot, about 3 minutes. Remove from the oven, divide the batter among the molds, and bake until the puddings have puffed up and formed a golden crust, 15–20 minutes.

5 Meanwhile, make the gravy: Pour off all but about 2 tablespoons of the drippings from the roasting pan and place on the stove top over medium heat. Using a wooden spoon, stir in the flour and cook until blended with the drippings, about 2 minutes. Add the wine, bring to a boil, and deglaze the pan, stirring to remove any browned bits from the pan bottom. Continue to stir vigorously until the mixture thickens into a paste, about 2 minutes. Immediately stir in the stock, increase the heat to medium-high, return to a boil, and cook, stirring, until thickened slightly, about 5 minutes. Season to taste, then strain the gravy through a fine-mesh sieve. Keep warm over low heat until ready to serve.

6 Just before the puddings are done, carve the roast and arrange on individual plates. Remove the puddings from the oven and, using the tip of a knife, lift from the molds, then divide among the plates. Pass the gravy and horseradish sauce at the table.

Serve with a full-bodied, spicy red Bordeaux from Saint-Emilion.

OMELET ARNOLD BENNETT

This omelet, which makes an ideal after-theater supper, was created in 1929 for Arnold Bennett while he was living in the Savoy Hotel on the Strand, researching the backstairs life of a luxury hotel for his novel Imperial Palace. *According to legend, he requested the same dish each night from the Savoy Grill: a smoked haddock and cheese omelet. Today, the Savoy Grill offers a luxuriously rich version topped with a glaze of reduced fish stock, Noilly Prat (vermouth), and cream. This recipe is simpler, but no less delicious.*

1 Preheat the broiler (grill). Cut the haddock or cod fillet in half and place the halves in a single layer in a nonreactive saucepan. Add the parsley, peppercorns, bay leaf, and milk. Bring to a boil over medium heat until bubbles start to appear around the edge of the pan. Reduce the heat to low and simmer until the fish flakes when a knife is inserted into the thickest part, 3–5 minutes. Using a slotted spoon, transfer the fish to a plate to cool. Discard the milk mixture.

2 When the fish is cool enough to handle, remove the skin. Break the flesh into rough flakes, discarding any small bones, and place in a small bowl. Stir in the cheese and season with pepper.

3 Set two 7-inch (18-cm) ovenproof omelet pans over medium-high heat and place 1 tablespoon butter in each pan. When the butter has melted, tilt the pans slightly to distribute the butter evenly. Pour half of the egg mixture into each pan. Repeatedly draw a wooden spoon through the egg mixture in each pan for about 1 minute until the bottom is set but the top is still liquid. Immediately cover the egg mixture in each pan with half of the fish mixture. Pour 2 tablespoons cream over the fish mixture in each pan. Place in the broiler and cook until the omelets are bubbling and flecked with brown, about 6 minutes.

4 Remove the pans from the broiler and slide the omelets onto warmed plates. Serve at once.

Serve with a buttery Italian Chardonnay from Piedmont or a white Burgundy.

½ lb (250 g) smoked haddock or smoked cod fillet

1 fresh flat-leaf (Italian) parsley sprig

3 peppercorns

1 fresh bay leaf

2 cups (16 fl oz/500 ml) whole milk

1 cup (4 oz/125 g) coarsely grated Gruyère cheese

Freshly ground pepper

2 tablespoons unsalted butter

4 large eggs, lightly beaten with a pinch of fine sea salt

4 tablespoons (2 fl oz/60 ml) heavy (double) cream

Coarsely snipped chives, for garnish

Makes 2 servings

London Smoked Fish

"London smoke" refers to a light, delicate style of smoked fish developed in the East End by Jewish immigrants. Fleeing their homes in eastern Europe from 1860 until 1905, they brought with them an expertise in curing fish, which they applied to two foods the British adored: haddock and salmon. Prior to this time, both fish were smoked in Scotland.

For many years, the East End was peppered with the chimneys of smokehouse brick kilns. With the arrival of inexpensive farmed Scottish salmon, small firms were unable to make a profit smoking the fish and gradually went out of business. H. Forman & Son, however, remained. Founded in 1905, the family-run smokehouse thrived by developing the upper end of the market. The salmon, both wild and farmed, is cured in salt, then smoked over smoldering oak chips. To expand the business, H. Forman & Son incorporated another old East End firm, F. & D. Lewzey, which specialized in smoking haddock, herring, and sprats. The plump haddock fillets are brined, spiked with sugar, and smoked over oak and beech sawdust. H. Forman & Son fish is sold in the top London food halls.

SEARED SCALLOPS WITH TAGLIATELLE, FAVA BEANS, AND BACON

Freshly picked fava beans in their velvety pods first appear in farmers' markets throughout London in June. Londoners eagerly take them home, shell the beans, and cook them briefly, then toss them into salads, purée them in creamy soups seasoned with sage, or add them to light pasta sauces like the one here. Bacon, a traditional British accompaniment to fava beans, enhances their sweetness. Pancetta, the Italian cured bacon, may be substituted. When selecting fava beans, try to find young, small beans as they will be more tender. It is important that the sauce be ready at the same time as the pasta.

1 cup (5 oz/155 g) shelled fava (broad) beans

1 lb (500 g) bay scallops or sea scallops

Fine sea salt

9 oz (280 g) dried tagliatelle or fettucine

8 tablespoons (4 fl oz/125 ml) extra-virgin olive oil

½ lb (250 g) lean bacon, diced

12 green (spring) onions, white and pale green parts only, thinly sliced

2 cloves garlic, finely chopped

Finely grated zest of 2 lemons

2 tablespoons fresh lemon juice

Freshly ground pepper

Makes 4 servings

1 Bring a small saucepan three-fourths full of water to a boil over high heat. Add the beans and boil for 3–4 minutes, or just until tender. Drain in a colander and run under cold water. If using large, older beans, pinch each bean to slip it from the skin. Discard the skins and set the beans aside.

2 Bring a pot three-fourths full of water to a boil over high heat. Remove any remaining tough, white muscle from the side of each scallop. If using sea scallops, cut them into quarters. Set aside.

3 Salt the boiling water, add the pasta, stir, and cook according to package directions until al dente.

4 While the pasta is cooking, in a frying pan over high heat, warm 3 tablespoons of the olive oil. Add the scallops and sear for 1 minute on each side. Remove from the pan and set aside. Add 3 tablespoons oil to the pan and reduce the heat to medium. Add the bacon and cook, stirring frequently, until it just begins to turn crisp, about 5 minutes. Stir in the green onions and garlic and cook until they begin to soften and become fragrant, about 1 minute. Add the beans, scallops, and lemon zest. Cook, stirring occasionally, until heated through, about 1 minute.

5 When the pasta is ready, drain and return to the pot. Add the remaining 2 tablespoons oil to the pasta and toss to coat. Add the lemon juice to the sauce and season with salt and pepper to taste. Add the sauce to the pasta, toss gently to combine, divide among warmed individual plates, and serve at once.

Serve with a full-bodied, dry white wine such as an Italian Verdicchio.

FISH PIE

This pie is a classic example of what the British refer to as "nursery food"—sophisticated nursery food for adults, who will find the seafood filling in a luscious sauce, topped with creamy mashed potatoes, very comforting. Traditional fish pies—known as "fish pies" regardless of their inclusion of shellfish—call for fresh white-fleshed fish, but this version also uses smoked haddock or cod to add a distinctive and appealing depth of flavor. The pie can be topped with puff pastry (see page 136) rather than mashed potatoes. In either case, petits pois, *tiny, sweet English peas, are a favorite accompaniment to this dish.*

1 To make the topping, place the potato chunks in a saucepan with cold water to cover generously and salt the water. Bring to a boil over medium heat and cook until the potatoes are tender when pierced with the tip of a knife, about 20 minutes. Drain in a colander, cover with a kitchen towel, and let stand until dry, about 5 minutes. For the fluffiest texture, pass the cooked potatoes through a ricer. Alternatively, place in a bowl and mash with a potato masher. Add the butter and beat until smooth. Pour in the milk and again beat until smooth. Season to taste with salt and pepper.

2 To make the filling, in a wide nonreactive saucepan over medium heat, combine the fresh fish fillets, milk, cream, peppercorns, parsley, and bay leaf. Bring to a simmer and cook until the fish flakes when a knife is inserted into the thickest part, 5–8 minutes. The timing will depend on the thickness of the fillets. Using a slotted spoon, transfer the fillets to a shallow bowl. Immerse the smoked fish fillets in the milk mixture, bring to a simmer over medium heat, and cook until the fish flakes when a knife is inserted into the thickest part, about 3 minutes. Using the slotted spoon, transfer the fillets to the shallow bowl. Strain the milk mixture and reserve. As the fish cools, add any liquid in the bowl to the strained milk mixture.

3 In a saucepan over low heat, melt the butter. Using a wooden spoon, stir in the flour and cook, stirring constantly, until blended with the butter, about 2 minutes. Stir in the vermouth, raise the heat to medium-high, and boil until the mixture is thick and

smooth, about 2 minutes. Slowly add the strained milk mixture, stirring constantly, and cook until a thick, smooth sauce forms, about 6 minutes. Reduce the heat to low and simmer until the flour has lost its raw taste, about 5 minutes. Remove the sauce from the heat, stir in the lemon juice, and season to taste with salt and pepper.

4 Preheat the oven to 375°F (190°C). Break the cooked fish into large flakes, discarding any small bones, and place in a large bowl. Peel and devein the shrimp. If using medium-sized shrimp, cut into bite-sized pieces. Remove any tough, white muscle from the side of each scallop. If using sea scallops, cut them in half. Add the scallops and shrimp to the bowl. Pour in the sauce and stir gently to combine. Divide the filling between six 1½-cup (12–fl oz/375-ml) baking dishes or ramekins or transfer to a 9-inch (23-cm) square baking dish about 3 inches (7.5 cm) deep. Top with the potato mixture, spreading it evenly to cover the filling. Using a fork, fluff the potatoes to create a textured surface.

5 Bake until the topping is golden and the filling is bubbling, about 30 minutes for individual pies and about 50 minutes for a single pie. Serve at once.

Serve with an herby, minerally white Burgundy such as Puligny-Montrachet.

FOR THE TOPPING

2 lb (1 kg) Yukon gold potatoes, peeled and cut into large chunks

Fine sea salt and ground pepper

⅓ cup (3 oz/90 g) unsalted butter, at room temperature

⅓ cup (3 fl oz/80 ml) whole milk

FOR THE FILLING

½ lb (250 g) fresh haddock or cod fillets, skin removed

1 cup (8 fl oz/250 ml) whole milk

⅔ cup (5 fl oz/160 ml) heavy (double) cream

5 peppercorns

3 flat-leaf (Italian) parsley sprigs

1 bay leaf

1½ lb (750 g) smoked haddock or cod fillets, skin removed

1 tablespoon unsalted butter

2 tablespoons all-purpose (plain) flour

⅔ cup (5 fl oz/160 ml) dry vermouth such as Noilly Prat

2 tablespoons fresh lemon juice

½ lb (250 g) *each* raw shrimp (prawns) and bay or sea scallops

Makes 6 servings

STEAMED SEA BASS WITH GINGER AND BLACK BEANS

Chinese immigrants have lived and worked around the docks in London's Limehouse since the 1850s. After the heavy bombing during World War II, they moved to Soho, where they were joined by farmers from Hong Kong. By the 1960s, Soho's Chinatown was thriving and became famous for its restaurants serving Cantonese food. The influence of Chinese cuisine has never abated. This recipe is an adaptation of a dish served at the Oriental Restaurant, which opened in 1990 at the Dorchester Hotel in Mayfair. Accompany the fish with steamed rice and stir-fried baby bok choy or Chinese greens.

1 tablespoon dried mandarin peel (see page 186), or 5 strips dried tangerine peel, about ½ inch (12 mm) wide and 1½ inches (4 cm) long

1 tablespoon sunflower oil

2 cloves garlic, peeled

2 tablespoons fermented black beans, chopped (see page 186)

2 tablespoons oyster sauce

1 tablespoon Chinese rice wine (see page 185) or dry sherry

1 tablespoon Asian sesame oil

¼ teaspoon corn oil

1 tablespoon sugar

1½ teaspoons cornstarch (cornflour) mixed with 3 tablespoons cold water

2 green (spring) onions, white and pale green parts only, thinly sliced on the diagonal

1 small red or green chile such as serrano, thinly sliced

½-inch (12-mm) piece fresh ginger, peeled and finely shredded

4 striped sea bass fillets, about 6–8 oz (185–250 g) each

Makes 4 servings

1 Place the mandarin peel in a small bowl, add cold water to cover, and let soak until soft, about 1 hour. Drain and finely chop. If using dried tangerine strips, grind them to a coarse powder in a mortar and pestle or an electric spice grinder. Set aside.

2 In a small saucepan over low heat, warm the sunflower oil. Add the garlic and cook for 1 minute; do not let the garlic turn brown. Add the black beans and cook gently until the beans are infused with the garlic oil, about 2 minutes. Remove from the heat and stir in the oyster sauce, rice wine, sesame oil, corn oil, sugar, and mandarin peel or tangerine peel. Bring to a boil over medium-high heat, reduce the heat to low, and simmer very gently until the flavors come together, about 10 minutes. Add the cornstarch mixture, stir vigorously, and simmer until thickened into a sauce, about 2 minutes. Pour the sauce into a nonreactive bowl and let cool, about 30 minutes.

3 Stir the green onions, chile, and ginger into the sauce. Add the fish fillets to the sauce and marinate for 10 minutes. Place 2 of the fillets, skin side down, in a single layer on a sheet of aluminum foil. Spoon half of the sauce over the fillets, turn to coat in the sauce, and arrange skin side down. Seal the foil tightly. Repeat with the 2 remaining fillets. Place the foil packets in separate compartments of a bamboo steamer or other steamer rack and cover tightly.

4 Pour water into a wok or other pan and bring to a boil. Place the steamer over the wok, and cook until the fish is opaque throughout and flakes when tested with a knife, about 12 minutes. Carefully remove the packets from the steamer. Gently unwrap and divide the fillets and the sauce between warmed plates. Serve at once.

Serve with a rose-scented white wine such as an Alsatian Gewürztraminer.

CHICKEN TIKKA MASALA

Indian food is so loved by the British that it is now regarded as an essential part of the national diet. The British developed a taste for curried dishes in the eighteenth century, but it was not until the 1970s that Indian restaurants began to influence how the British ate. Soon, every neighborhood had an Indian restaurant where residents could enjoy a meal or order their favorite takeaway. One of the most popular dishes, a uniquely British invention, is chicken tikka masala, succulent cubes of chicken breast bathed in a sweet, spicy sauce.

1 In a nonreactive bowl, stir together the yogurt, lime juice, 2 teaspoons ginger, cumin, garam masala, and paprika. Trim excess fat from the chicken and cut into 1-inch (2.5-cm) cubes. Add to the marinade, stir, cover, and refrigerate for at least 1 hour or up to 7 hours.

2 Preheat the broiler (grill). Remove the chicken from the marinade, shaking off the excess, and place on a plate. Season with salt and drizzle with 2 tablespoons sunflower oil; toss to coat. Arrange the chicken in a single layer on a foil-lined broiler pan set just below the broiler and broil (grill), turning once, until browned, 3 minutes on each side. Alternatively, heat a stove-top grill pan over medium-high heat, add the chicken in a single layer, and cook, turning once, until browned, 3 minutes on each side. Set aside.

3 To make the masala sauce, in a saucepan over medium heat, warm the remaining 3 tablespoons sunflower oil. Add the onion, remaining 1 teaspoon ginger, and garlic and cook, stirring frequently, until the onion is soft, 4–5 minutes. Add the cardamom, cumin, coriander, turmeric, and ground chili and cook, stirring constantly, for 2 minutes. Add the tomatoes and cook, stirring frequently, until the oil separates from the tomato mixture, 5–8 minutes. Add the chile, cream, and ½ cup (4 fl oz/125 ml) water, bring to a boil, reduce the heat to low, and simmer until the mixture forms a creamy sauce, 8–10 minutes. Stir in the cooked chicken and the garam masala, season to taste with salt, and simmer until the chicken is heated, 8–10 minutes. Stir in the lemon juice. Serve at once with warm naan or pita breads.

¼ cup (2 oz/60 g) Greek yogurt or other plain whole-milk yogurt

Juice of 1½ limes

3 teaspoons peeled and finely chopped fresh ginger

1 teaspoon *each* ground cumin and garam masala

2 teaspoons paprika

4 skinless, boneless chicken breast halves, about 4 oz (125 g) each

Fine sea salt

5 tablespoons (2½ fl oz/75 ml) sunflower oil

1 small yellow onion, finely diced

1 clove garlic, finely chopped

5 green cardamom pods

1 teaspoon *each* ground cumin and ground coriander

½ teaspoon *each* ground turmeric and ground chile

1 lb (500 g) tomatoes, peeled, seeded, and diced (see page 187)

1 jalapeño chile, thinly sliced

½ cup (4 fl oz/125 ml) heavy (double) cream

¼ teaspoon garam masala

Juice of ½ lemon

Warm naan or pita breads

Makes 4 servings

Indian Shops

When shoppers step into grocers such as Nita Cash & Carry in Wembley, the scent of joss sticks mingling with the aroma of spices and sandalwood immediately transports them to India. Bags of lentils for dal, sacks of chapati flour and basmati rice, *tavas* (griddle pans), and *thalis* (metal serving plates with bowls) fill the shelves. Outside are colorful displays of fruits and vegetables such as green mangoes and bitter melons for pickling. Customers and shopkeepers haggle over fragrant guavas, bunches of fenugreek, and gleaming green chiles until all are happy with the price.

It is possible to travel the Indian subcontinent while wandering around London. Brick Lane is predominantly Bangladeshi, Southall is Punjabi, and Wembley is Gujarati, while Tooting has a mix of Sri Lankans, Pakistanis, and East Africans. Each neighborhood has its own shops, restaurants, temples, and mosques. There are also many smaller communities, such as Drummond Street behind Euston Station. Shoppers here buy Indian and Pakistani sweets and snacks for festivals and weddings from the Ambala Sweet Centre on Drummond Street.

SPRING LAMB WITH RAITA, MINT, AND GREEN ONIONS

One of the first signs of spring in London is the arrival of delicate, rosy pink cuts of spring lamb from the green hills of Dorset, which appear in butcher shops every March. As the summer progresses, lamb is brought in from farther north. Come September, the hill breeds of Scotland and Northumberland are ready for eating. These tender cuts are ideally suited to Londoners, who prefer quick-grilled or roasted meats. Roast lamb is often served with mint sauce or red currant jelly. This recipe is an upscale version of a kebab, a dish young Londoners eat when out on the town and in need of a tasty, inexpensive snack.

FOR THE MARINADE

1 large yellow onion

Juice of 1 large lemon

Extra-virgin olive oil for brushing

Freshly ground pepper

2 lb (1 kg) boneless, lean lamb from loin or leg, cut into 1-inch (2.5-cm) cubes

Extra-virgin olive oil for brushing

FOR THE RAITA

1½ cups (12 oz/375 g) Greek yogurt or other plain whole-milk yogurt

½ English (hothouse) cucumber, peeled and coarsely shredded

Fine sea salt and freshly ground pepper

FOR THE SALAD

6 green (spring) onions, white parts only, thinly sliced

¼ cup (⅓ oz/10 g) fresh mint leaves, coarsely shredded

2 hearts of romaine (cos) lettuce, coarsely shredded

4 large or 8 small pita breads

Makes 4 servings

1 To make the marinade, coarsely grate the onion into a fine-mesh sieve set over a large bowl. Press on the onion with the back of a wooden spoon to extract as much juice as possible. Discard the grated onion. Add the lemon juice and olive oil to the onion juice and season with pepper. Add the lamb cubes, turn to coat, cover with plastic wrap, and refrigerate for at least 2 hours or up to 8 hours.

2 To make the raita, put the yogurt in a serving bowl. If using Greek yogurt, whisk in ½ cup (4 fl oz/ 125 ml) cold water to form a creamy, thick sauce. Add the cucumber, season to taste with salt and pepper, and stir to combine. Cover and refrigerate until needed.

3 Prepare a charcoal or gas grill for direct grilling over medium-high heat. If using wooden skewers, soak them in water for 30 minutes.

4 To make the salad, in a bowl, combine the green onions, mint, and romaine. Set aside.

5 Remove the lamb cubes from the marinade. Thread the cubes on the skewers. Season with salt and brush with olive oil. Place the skewers on the grill rack directly over the heat and grill, turning frequently, until deep brown, 4–6 minutes for medium-rare. Alternatively, place a stove-top grill pan over medium-high heat. When it is hot, add the skewers and cook the meat, turning frequently, for 4–6 minutes for medium-rare. Remove the cubes from the skewers and add to the salad.

6 Set the pita breads on the grill rack or grill pan and grill, turning once, until warm, 2–3 minutes. Split open each pita bread and fill with the salad and lamb. Spoon on some of the raita and serve at once.

Serve with a pale rosé from Côtes de Provence or a rosato from southern Italy.

PUDDINGS

Rhubarb fool, peach and raspberry trifle, and sticky toffee pudding

reflect the passing seasons in London as surely as the changing weather.

In Britain, dessert refers to a course of nuts and dried or sugared fruit offered with Port at the end of a meal. Puddings, a peculiarly British term, connotes sweet dishes served after the main course. Emphasis is on the best seasonal fruits, from juicy apricots in a midsummer crumble to luxurious dates in a steamed winter pudding. At restaurants, elegance is the keynote—such as a warm pear soufflé or a panna cotta flavored with rose water and garnished with apples and dried fruit. Home cooks favor such simple dishes as summer pudding with mixed berries or hazelnut meringue with juicy blackberries and cream.

HAZELNUT MERINGUE WITH BLACKBERRIES AND CREAM

A crisp meringue covered in lashings of thickly whipped cream and dewy blackberries makes the perfect dessert for a warm September day. Blackberries, although they are an indigenous fruit, appear rarely in British cookbooks. This is probably because they were regarded as a cheap food best suited for working-class Londoners who used to take their families out brambling in the surrounding countryside. They filled every conceivable container with blackberries and brought them home to mix with coarse brown sugar for jam. Today's urban cooks buy cultivated blackberries from markets to make pies, crumbles, and mousses.

1 To make the meringue, preheat the oven to 350°F (180°C). Spread the hazelnuts on a baking sheet and toast until the skins start to wrinkle and flake off, about 15 minutes. Transfer to a plate. When the nuts are cool enough to handle, pour them onto a kitchen towel and rub vigorously to remove the skins. Not every speck will come off. Place the hazelnuts in a food processor and pulse 3 or 4 times until they form very fine crumbs. Set aside.

2 Draw an 8-inch (20-cm) circle on a piece of parchment (baking) paper and place on a baking sheet. Put the egg whites in a large, clean bowl. Using a balloon whisk or an electric mixer on medium speed, beat until the whites begin to thicken. Continue to beat, increasing the speed to medium-high if using an electric mixer, just until soft peaks form. Slowly add the superfine sugar and continue to beat until medium-firm peaks form. Be careful not to overbeat the whites

or they may start to separate. Sprinkle in the vinegar, salt, and cornstarch and fold in with a metal spoon. Fold in the ground hazelnuts until incorporated. Spoon the mixture inside the circle on the prepared baking sheet. Using the metal spoon, neatly shape and flatten into a disk. Place in the oven, reduce the temperature to 300°F (150°C), and bake for 1 hour. Turn off the heat and leave the meringue in the oven until cold, about 3 hours. The outside will be crisp, and the inside will be soft and chewy. Transfer the cold hazelnut meringue to a serving plate.

3 To make the topping, in a large bowl, combine the cream and kirsch, if using. Using a whisk or handheld mixer, whip until soft peaks form. Spoon over the meringue and scatter the blackberries on top. Dust with superfine sugar, cut into wedges, and serve.

FOR THE MERINGUE

⅓ cup (2 oz/60 g) hazelnuts (filberts)

3 large egg whites, at room temperature

¾ cup (5 oz/155 g) superfine (caster) sugar

½ teaspoon white wine vinegar

Pinch of fine sea salt

1 teaspoon cornstarch (cornflour)

FOR THE TOPPING

1 cup (8 fl oz/250 ml) heavy (double) cream

3 tablespoons kirsch (optional)

3 cups (12 oz/375 g) blackberries

Superfine (caster) sugar for dusting

Makes 6 servings

SUMMER PUDDING

By July, when markets are piled high with punnets of strawberries, raspberries, and currants, few cooks can resist making a summer pudding. The scent of the warm berries is so enticing that it takes discipline to resist turning out the pudding before it sets. The key to success is to use a good-quality white bread from a local bakery. The bread should have sufficient body to absorb the juice of the cooked fruits and hold its shape, despite being cut into thin slices. If fresh currants are unavailable, do not substitute dried. Instead, replace them with blackberries or blueberries and adjust the sugar to taste.

2 cups (8 oz/250 g) red currants, stems removed

2 cups (8 oz/250 g) black currants, stems removed

4 cups (1 lb/500 g) strawberries, hulled and halved

1½ cups (12 oz/375 g) sugar

3 tablespoons raspberry or strawberry eau-de-vie (optional)

2 cups (8 oz/250 g) raspberries, plus more for garnish

Canola or sunflower oil

8–10 slices good-quality, firm white bread, about ¼ inch (6 mm) thick, crusts removed (see note)

Fresh mint leaves for garnish (optional)

1 cup (8 fl oz/250 ml) heavy (double) cream for serving

Makes 6 servings

1 In a nonreactive saucepan, combine the red and black currants, strawberries, and sugar. Add the eau-de-vie, if desired, or 3 tablespoons water. Cover, place over low heat, and cook, stirring occasionally, until the sugar is dissolved and the fruit releases plenty of juice, about 5 minutes. Stir in the 2 cups raspberries and cook, covered, until the raspberries just begin to release their juices, about 2 minutes. Let cool while you prepare the pudding basin. The fruit will continue to release juice as it cools.

2 Lightly oil a 3-cup (24–fl oz/250-ml) pudding basin or ceramic or glass bowl with a 6-inch (15-cm) diameter rim and a 3-inch (7-cm) diameter base. Cut out a circle of bread that will fit in the bottom of the basin, and place in the basin. Cut out another circle that will fit inside the top, and set aside. Cut the remaining bread slices into wedges or triangles and use them to line the sides of the basin, making sure that there are no gaps between the pieces. The bread slices should extend above the rim of the basin.

3 Spoon the fruit into the bread-lined basin, packing it gently. It should come to ½ inch (12 mm) below the rim of the basin. Reserve any extra fruit and juice in a covered container in the refrigerator until ready to serve. Seal the fruit in by folding over the bread that

extends above the rim of the basin over the fruit filling. Cover with the remaining reserved circle of bread, pressing down gently. Set a saucer on top of the bread circle and weight with a heavy can. Place the basin in a dish to catch any juices and refrigerate for at least 8 hours or up to 2 days.

4 Remove the weight and saucer from the top of the pudding. Run a sharp knife along the inside of the bowl, being careful not to cut into the pudding. Invert a plate on top of the basin, invert the plate and basin together, shake the basin sharply, and then carefully lift off the basin. Pour any reserved juices over the pudding so that it looks glossy.

5 To serve, garnish the pudding with the reserved fruit or fresh berries and mint leaves, if desired. Pass the cream at the table.

Serve with a well-chilled sparkling Italian dessert wine such as Freisa or a perfumed white wine such as Malvasia from Piedmont.

PEACH AND RASPBERRY TRIFLE

A trifle made from sponge cake, seasonal fruit, homemade custard, and cream epitomizes London summer chic. Each element is delicious on its own, but when combined, they become an exquisite dessert. The earliest recorded recipes date to the sixteenth century, when trifles and desserts such as syllabubs and fools were interchangeable. A classic trifle is simply a layer each of cake, jam, custard, and cream often served in a large bowl. Modern trifles are updated with crushed macaroons or fresh fruit. This contemporary version, served in individual cups, has multiple layers of sponge cake, summer fruit, and custard.

1 To make the sponge cake, preheat the oven to 375°F (190°C). Line an 8-by-12-inch (20-by-30-cm) baking sheet with parchment (baking) paper and lightly oil the paper. In a large bowl, using an electric mixer, whisk together the eggs and ⅓ cup superfine sugar until pale and thick, about 5 minutes. Using a metal spoon, fold in the flour and salt. Pour into the prepared baking sheet and spread evenly. Bake until the cake is golden and springs back when lightly touched with a fingertip, about 10 minutes.

2 Generously sprinkle superfine sugar on a sheet of parchment paper that is slightly larger than the sponge cake. Carefully run a small, thin knife around the inside of the pan to loosen the cake. Invert onto the sugar-coated parchment and lift off the pan. Peel off the paper and let cool to room temperature.

3 Have ready six 1½-cup (12–fl oz/375-ml) tall dessert glasses or bowls. Using a serrated knife, trim the edges of the sponge cake, then cut into 18 pieces that will fit inside the dessert glasses. Wrap the pieces with plastic wrap and set aside.

4 To make the custard, in a small saucepan, combine the milk, vanilla bean, and granulated sugar. Set over low heat and cook, stirring occasionally, until the sugar is dissolved, about 10 minutes. Increase the heat to medium. As soon as small bubbles appear along the edge of the pan, about 2 minutes, remove the pan from the heat. Let steep for 20 minutes.

5 In a bowl, whisk the egg yolks until smooth, about 1 minute. Remove the vanilla bean from the milk

and reserve. Whisking constantly, slowly pour the warm milk into the eggs. Return to the saucepan, add the vanilla bean, set over low heat, and cook, stirring constantly with a wooden spoon, until the custard thickens enough to coat the back of the spoon, 10–20 minutes. Do not let the custard boil. Strain the custard through a fine-mesh sieve into a bowl. Stir until the custard cools slightly, about 10 minutes. Cover with plastic wrap, pressing it onto the surface of the custard to prevent a skin from forming, and refrigerate until chilled, at least 1 hour or up to 2 days.

6 To prepare the fruit, in a nonreactive bowl, combine the liqueur and lemon juice. Working over the bowl to catch the juices, cut the peaches into thin slices and let them drop into the bowl. Add the raspberries and stir gently to combine. Set aside for at least 30 minutes or up to 3 hours.

7 Crumble 1 cake piece into the bottom of each dessert glass. Spoon 1 tablespoon of fruit mixture over the cake in each bowl and drizzle a little fruit juice over the cake. Drizzle 2 tablespoons of custard over the fruit. Repeat with a layer of cake and a second layer of fruit and custard. Top the layers with a third piece of cake, then a third layer of fruit and custard. Cover with plastic wrap and refrigerate for 30 minutes.

8 Just before serving, pour the cream into a large bowl. Using a whisk or handheld mixer, whip the cream until soft peaks form. Garnish the top of each trifle with a large dollop of whipped cream. Sprinkle with pistachios, if desired, and serve.

FOR THE SPONGE CAKE

2 large eggs

⅓ cup (2½ oz/75 g) superfine (caster) sugar, plus more for sprinkling

⅓ cup (2 oz/60 g) all-purpose (plain) flour, sifted

Pinch of fine sea salt

FOR THE CUSTARD

1¾ cups (14 fl oz/430 ml) whole milk

1 vanilla bean, split in half lengthwise

½ cup (4 oz/125 g) granulated sugar

6 large egg yolks

FOR THE FRUIT

½ cup (4 fl oz/120 ml) orange liqueur such as Grand Marnier

1 tablespoon fresh lemon juice

2 ripe peaches, peeled

1 cup (4 oz/125 g) raspberries

1 cup (8 fl oz/250 ml) chilled heavy (double) cream

2 tablespoons coarsely chopped pistachio nuts (optional)

Makes 6 servings

TREACLE TART

The sticky, sweet character of treacle tart has made it a favorite in gentlemen's clubs and traditional eating establishments for at least a hundred years. In Britain the term treacle *usually refers to old-fashioned black treacle or molasses, both products of sugar refining. Despite its misleading name, treacle tart filling is made with soft white bread crumbs soaked in golden syrup and citrus. Golden syrup, introduced in 1883, has an 80 percent sugar content along with a clear golden color and a delicate taste. Some markets outside Britain carry the syrup, especially Lyle's, but if it is unavailable, corn syrup may be substituted.*

FOR THE PASTRY

2 cups (10 oz/315 g) all-purpose (plain) flour

Pinch of fine sea salt

¾ cup (6 oz/185 g) cold unsalted butter, diced

5–6 tablespoons (2½–3 fl oz/ 74–90 ml) cold water

FOR THE FILLING

2 cups (16 fl oz/500 ml) golden syrup or light corn syrup, or as needed

2⅔ cups (5½ oz/170 g) fresh white bread crumbs

Finely grated zest of 2 lemons

Finely grated zest of 1 orange

2 tablespoons fresh lemon juice

1 teaspoon ground ginger

1 cup (8 fl oz/250 ml) heavy (double) cream for serving

Makes 8 servings

1 To make the pastry, combine the flour and salt in a large bowl. Using a pastry blender or 2 knives, cut in the butter until the mixture forms coarse crumbs. Alternatively, place the flour and salt in a food processor, add the butter, and pulse 4 or 5 times until the mixture forms coarse crumbs; transfer to a bowl. Using a fork, stir in enough of the cold water to form a rough dough. Turn the dough out onto a lightly floured work surface and lightly knead just until smooth, about 30 seconds. Shape the dough into a disk ¾ inch (2 cm) thick, wrap tightly in plastic wrap, and refrigerate for at least 30 minutes or up to overnight.

2 Preheat the oven to 400°F (200°C). On a lightly floured work surface, roll out two-thirds of the dough into a 9-inch (25-cm) round ⅛ inch (3 mm) thick. Drape the dough over the rolling pin and ease into a 7-inch (18-cm) tart pan with a removable bottom, pressing it into place and leaving the overhang. Use a rolling pin to roll over the edge of the tart pan to cut off the excess pastry overhang. Prick the dough with a fork in several places and refrigerate for 30 minutes. Add the trimmings to the remaining dough and press together into a disk. Wrap in plastic wrap and refrigerate until needed.

3 To make the filling, in a nonreactive saucepan over low heat, warm 1½ cups (12 fl oz/375 ml) of the golden syrup until it thins and becomes more liquid. Remove from the heat and stir in the bread

crumbs, lemon and orange zests, lemon juice, and ginger. Let stand until the bread crumbs absorb the liquid, about 10 minutes. The mixture should be soft and sticky rather than stiff and thick or thin and runny. Add the remaining ½ cup (4 fl oz/125 ml) golden syrup, if necessary, until the mixture reaches the right consistency. Spoon into the pastry-lined pan.

4 On a lightly floured work surface, roll out the remaining dough into a rectangle about 7 inches (18 cm) long, 5 inches (13 cm) wide, and ⅛ inch (3 mm) thick. Trim the edges. Cut lengthwise into 10 strips about ½ inch (12 mm) wide. Lay 5 of the strips, evenly spaced, over the filling. Lay the remaining 5 strips, evenly spaced, perpendicular across the first 5 strips. Trim the excess dough and crimp to seal the edges.

5 Bake for 10 minutes. Reduce the oven temperature to 350°F (180°C) and bake until the pastry is golden, about 15 minutes. Transfer to a wire rack to cool slightly. Remove the tart pan ring and transfer to a serving plate or stand. Serve warm or cold, cut into wedges, with cream.

Serve with a nutty, maple-scented dessert wine such as Malmsey Madeira or tawny Port.

STRAWBERRY PAIN PERDU

Pain perdu, *French for "lost bread," has been enjoying a revival, no doubt because it is both delicious and easy to make. Its origins date to the Middle Ages when slices of brioche or fine white bread were soaked in egg yolks, fried until crisp in clarified butter, then liberally sprinkled with sugar. Over the centuries, cinnamon, nutmeg, and other spices have been added, along with alcohol, such as sack, a white wine from Spain, and even cream. More recently, cooks have taken to accompanying* pain perdu *with berries or fried bananas.*

1 In a bowl, combine the strawberries and the confectioners' sugar. Toss gently and set aside.

2 In a large shallow bowl, whisk together the egg yolks, sherry, superfine sugar, and nutmeg. Soak the brioche slices in the egg yolk mixture for 1 minute, turning them at least once.

3 Meanwhile, in a large nonstick frying pan over medium heat, warm the clarified butter. Remove the brioche slices from the egg yolk mixture. Place the slices in the pan and cook until golden and slightly crisp, about 2 minutes. Turn and cook until golden and slightly crisp on the second side, 1–2 minutes.

4 Divide the slices among 4 individual plates. Top with the strawberries, garnish with a dollop of crème fraîche, if desired, and serve at once.

Serve with a glass of pink Champagne or a Banyuls from France's Roussillon region.

4 cups (1 lb/500 g) strawberries, hulled and halved

3 tablespoons confectioners' (icing) sugar

4 large egg yolks

¼ cup (2 fl oz/60 ml) dry sherry

1 tablespoon superfine (caster) sugar

Pinch of freshly grated nutmeg

4 slices brioche loaf, about ½ inch (12 mm) thick, cut in half diagonally

2 tablespoons clarified unsalted butter (see page 185)

¼ cup (2 oz/60 g) crème fraîche for serving (optional)

Makes 4 servings

English Strawberries

By early summer, the London air is sweet with the scent of flowers. The first English strawberries appear in the shops, and Champagne goes on special offer. The summer social season gets started with the Chelsea Flower Show in May and continues with racing at Royal Ascot, tennis at Wimbledon, and rowing at Henley Royal Regatta. Each event calls for dressing up, having fun, and eating delectable food. And no occasion is considered complete without strawberries, preferably accompanied by lashings of cream and a generous sprinkling of sugar. Newspapers even comment on the price of a bowl of strawberries at Wimbledon.

Strawberries have long been sold in London. In medieval times, wild fruit was picked, strung on pieces of straw, and hawked on the streets. By the seventeenth century, new varieties such as the small Hautbois from France and the wild Virginia strawberry from America graced fashionable London tables. Then, in the early nineteenth century, market gardeners like Michael Keens in Isleworth began to create ever bigger hybrids. The French called these large strawberries *les fraises anglaises*.

ROSE WATER PANNA COTTA WITH APPLE COMPOTE

Eating a trembly, creamy panna cotta with seasonal fruit is most Londoners' idea of gustatory bliss. Here, both the panna cotta and the apple compote are subtly scented with rose water, a favorite British flavoring since medieval times. British cooks often add floral notes to puddings and syrups, infusing them with elderflowers in spring, lavender flowers in summer, and orange flower water throughout the year. In the autumn, cooks turn to seasonal apples, pears, and quince to use in their puddings. Apple varieties that maintain their shape when cooked, such as Braeburn, are best for this compote.

FOR THE PANNA COTTA

3 cups (24 fl oz/750 ml) heavy (double) cream

2 cups (16 fl oz/500 ml) whole milk

3 lemon zest strips

1 tablespoon unflavored gelatin

²⁄₃ cup (4½ oz/140 g) superfine (caster) sugar

2 teaspoons distilled rose water

2 tablespoons white dessert wine such as Muscat de Beaumes de Venise

FOR THE APPLE COMPOTE

½ cup (4 oz/125 g) granulated sugar

Finely grated zest of 1 lemon

1 teaspoon distilled rose water

2 apples, peeled, cored, and diced (see note)

2 tablespoons dried cranberries

2 tablespoons dried blueberries

2 tablespoons dried cherries

2 tablespoons fresh lemon juice

Makes 6 servings

1 To make the panna cotta, in a wide nonreactive saucepan, combine the cream, milk, and lemon zest. Set over medium-low heat, warm the liquid just until small bubbles appear along the edge of the pan, then reduce the heat to low and simmer gently until reduced by about one-fifth, about 15 minutes.

2 Meanwhile, place 3 tablespoons water in a large bowl, sprinkle the gelatin over the water, and let soften for about 5 minutes. Pour the hot cream mixture through a fine-mesh sieve into the bowl and stir to dissolve the gelatin. Add the superfine sugar and stir until dissolved. Stir in the rose water and wine.

3 Lightly oil six ¾-cup (6–fl oz/180-ml) custard cups. Divide the mixture evenly among the prepared molds. Cover and refrigerate until firm, at least 6 hours or up to overnight.

4 To make the apple compote, in a nonreactive saucepan over medium heat, combine the granulated sugar, lemon zest, and ½ cup (4 fl oz/ 125 ml) water. Cook, stirring occasionally, until the sugar is dissolved. Simmer until the mixture thickens

and becomes syrupy, about 5 minutes. Add the rose water, apples, and dried cranberries, blueberries, and cherries, reduce the heat to low, and simmer just until the apples are tender, about 5 minutes. Remove from the heat, stir in the lemon juice, and transfer to a serving bowl. Let cool to room temperature.

5 To unmold each panna cotta, place the custard cup in a bowl of hot water for about 10 seconds. Invert a dessert plate on top of the custard cup and invert the custard cup and plate together. Shake the mold gently to loosen the panna cotta. Spoon the apple compote around and over the top of each panna cotta, dividing it evenly. Serve at once.

Serve with a sweet, perfumed white wine such as Muscat de Beaumes-de-Venise.

RHUBARB FOOL

Every January, the first pale pink stalks of forced Yorkshire rhubarb appear in London. The plants are forced by transplanting them from the cold Yorkshire ground into warm, dark growing sheds, where they are picked by candlelight until the end of the season in early March. With their fine taste and texture, the slender spears are considered a delicacy. Chefs and home cooks eagerly make rhubarb tarts, pies, crumbles, and jellies, but rhubarb fool, the stewed fruit folded into whipped cream, is what everyone likes best. Fools are usually accompanied by small biscuits, such as almond cookies or ladyfingers.

1 Trim the ends of the rhubarb and cut into 1-inch (2.5-cm) pieces. In a nonreactive saucepan, combine the rhubarb, sugar, and 2 tablespoons water. Set over medium heat and cook, stirring occasionally, until the rhubarb begins to release its juice and the sugar is dissolved, about 2 minutes. Reduce the heat to low, cover, and simmer until the rhubarb is tender and almost completely disintegrated, 5–8 minutes. Remove from the heat and let cool to room temperature for about 1 hour.

2 In a large bowl, combine the cream and Cointreau (if using). Using a whisk or handheld mixer, whip until soft peaks form. Using a metal spoon, fold in the cooked rhubarb and its juice so that pink ripples are created through the cream.

3 Divide the rhubarb mixture among stemmed bowls and refrigerate for at least 1 hour before serving.

Serve with a chilled Italian sparkling wine such as Prosecco or Freisa.

1 lb (500 g) rhubarb

1 cup (8 oz/250 g) sugar

1 cup (8 fl oz/250 g) very cold heavy (double) cream

3 tablespoons Cointreau (optional)

Makes 6 servings

STICKY TOFFEE PUDDING

Steamed puddings became fashionable in the seventeenth century with the invention of the pudding cloth, a piece of fabric that was tied around the uncooked pudding, allowing it to be boiled in a pot. In the nineteenth century, wooden and china pudding basins replaced the cloth, and today, cooks primarily use china basins. Whether sweet or savory, puddings often contained spices and "plums," which referred to any variety of dried fruit. Initially, they were moistened with eggs, suet, or marrow, but by the nineteenth century, rising agents were used to create light puddings, such as this one studded with dates.

FOR THE DATE PUDDING

½ lb (250 g) pitted Medjool dates, finely chopped

½ cup (4 fl oz/125 ml) very hot black tea such as Earl Grey

1¼ cups (6½ oz/200 g) all-purpose (plain) flour

1 teaspoon baking powder

⅓ cup (3 oz/90 g) unsalted butter, at room temperature

¾ cup (6 oz/185 g) firmly packed light brown sugar

½ teaspoon vanilla extract (essence)

2 large eggs

1 tablespoon Cognac

FOR THE TOFFEE SAUCE

1 cup (7 oz/220 g) firmly packed light brown sugar

½ cup (4 oz/125 g) unsalted butter

⅓ cup (3 fl oz/90 ml) heavy (double) cream

2 tablespoons Cognac

Pinch of fine sea salt

Makes 6 servings

1 To make the pudding, in a small bowl, combine the chopped dates and hot tea. Let soak for 30 minutes.

2 Generously butter six ¾-cup (6–fl oz/180 ml) individual custard cups or a 4½-cup (36–fl oz/1.1-l) pudding basin. Cut out circles of baking (parchment) paper that will fit the top and bottom of the mold(s). Place the bottom circle(s) in the mold(s). Select a wide, covered saucepan that will comfortably hold the mold(s) and fill with enough water to reach two-thirds of the way up the side of the mold(s). Remove the mold(s) and bring the water to a boil.

3 Sift the flour and baking powder into a bowl and set aside. In a separate bowl, using an electric mixer on medium-high speed, beat the butter and brown sugar until fluffy, about 2 minutes. Beat in the vanilla. Add the eggs and Cognac and beat until pale and fluffy. Add the flour mixture and beat on low speed just until incorporated. Using a wooden spoon, stir in the dates and any soaking liquid.

4 Spoon the mixture into the prepared mold(s). Cover with the remaining circle(s) of paper. Cut squares of aluminum foil larger than the diameter of the mold(s). Fold to create a pleat in the center to allow the pudding to rise as it cooks. Place over the top(s) of the mold(s) and wrap around the rim to form a tight lid.

5 Carefully lower the mold(s) into the pan of boiling water, cover, and boil steadily until a knife inserted in the center comes out clean, about 45 minutes for the individual cups or 2 hours for the pudding basin. Check the water level occasionally and add more water if it starts to get too low. Carefully remove the mold(s) from the saucepan and let stand for 10 minutes.

6 While the pudding is resting, make the sauce: In a small saucepan over low heat, combine the brown sugar, butter, cream, Cognac, and salt. Cook, stirring occasionally, until the sugar is dissolved and the butter is melted, about 4 minutes. Raise the heat to medium-high, bring to a boil, and cook, stirring frequently, until the sauce has thickened and darkened and tastes of toffee, about 4 minutes.

7 Remove the foil and parchment paper circle(s) from the mold(s). Run a sharp knife around the edge of the pudding. Invert a plate on top of a cup or the basin and invert the plate and cup or basin together. Shake the cup or basin sharply, and lift off. Peel off the remaining circle of paper. Pour some of the warm sauce over the pudding. Serve at once with the remaining sauce.

Serve with a rich, complex sweet dessert wine such as Madeira or tawny Port.

OAT CAKES WITH CHEESE AND CELERY

Londoners are spoiled by the array of superb cheeses they can buy in specialist shops such as Neal's Yard Dairy or La Fromagerie. Traditionally, cheese is served as a separate course before, after, or instead of the pudding. In each case, the preferred accompaniments are a selection of plain biscuits, such as oat cakes, water biscuits, or Bath Olivers, and crisp celery. Freshly baked oat cakes are particularly delicious when smeared with a lemony fresh goat's milk cheese, a British blue cheese such as Stilton, a crumbly cow's milk cheese such as Wensleydale, or the Devonshire sheep's milk cheese Beenleigh Blue.

1 Preheat the oven to 375°F (190°C). Line 2 baking sheets with parchment (baking) paper.

2 In a bowl, stir together the oat flour, all-purpose flour, baking soda, and salt. Using a wooden spoon, stir in the melted butter and warm water. Using your hands, mix to form a stiff, slightly sticky dough, about 2 minutes. The dough should be pliant enough to roll; if necessary, sprinkle on a little more warm water and mix in with your hands.

3 Turn the dough out onto a lightly floured work surface. Dust a rolling pin with flour and roll out the dough into a round ⅛ inch (3 mm) thick. If the dough keeps breaking up, return it to the bowl, add a few more drops of warm water, and mix again with your hands. Dust a 2¼-inch (5.5-cm) cookie cutter with flour and, using a quick, sharp motion, cut out oat cakes as close together as possible. Gather the scraps of dough, roll out, and cut additional cakes. Place the cakes 1 inch (2.5 cm) apart on the prepared baking sheets. Bake until the oat cakes are lightly colored and crisp, about 12 minutes. Transfer to a wire rack to cool. The cakes can be stored in an airtight container for up to a month.

4 Meanwhile, about 15 minutes before serving, arrange the cheeses on a cheeseboard or a platter and allow to come to room temperature. Transfer the oat cakes to a serving platter with the celery and allow guests to help themselves.

1⅓ cups (4 oz/125 g) oat flour (medium-grind oatmeal)

1 tablespoon all-purpose (plain) flour

½ teaspoon baking soda (bicarbonate of soda)

¼ teaspoon fine sea salt

1½ tablespoons unsalted butter, melted

½ cup (4 fl oz/125 ml) warm water, or as needed

A selection of cheeses, such as fresh goat cheese, blue-veined cheese, and aged cow's or sheep's milk cheese (see note)

1 bunch celery, separated into stalks and trimmed

Makes 4–6 servings

APRICOT-ALMOND CRUMBLE

No gastropub menu is complete without a crumble. Seasonal fruit is baked until the juices bubble through the delicate crumbling crust. In early summer, apricots begin to appear in London shops, soon followed by juicy peaches and cherries. Apricots are often flavored with rose water or with vanilla bean, as in this recipe. No one knows who invented the crumble, but it first appeared in British cookbooks in the mid-twentieth century. The recipe may have been developed in response to wartime rationing and the lack of time to make complicated desserts.

FOR THE TOPPING

1½ cups (7½ oz/235 g) all-purpose (plain) flour

⅓ cup (2 oz/60 g) whole unblanched almonds

½ cup (4 oz/125 g) cold unsalted butter, finely diced

⅓ cup (2½ oz/75 g) superfine (caster) sugar

2½ lb (1.25 kg) apricots, halved and pitted

1 cup (8 oz/250 g) granulated sugar

1 vanilla bean, halved lengthwise and cut in half crosswise

Makes 6 servings

1 Preheat the oven to 400°F (200°C). To make the topping, place the flour and almonds in a food processor. Pulse repeatedly until the nuts form very fine crumbs in the flour. Add the butter and pulse 3 or 4 times until the mixture forms crumbs the size of fine bread crumbs. Transfer to a bowl and stir in the superfine sugar.

2 In a 9-by-2½ inch (23-by-6 cm) round or oval baking dish or pie dish, stir together the apricots and granulated sugar. Insert the pieces of vanilla bean in the fruit. Sprinkle the topping evenly over the fruit and lightly pat down.

3 Bake until the topping firms up and begins to brown, about 25 minutes. Reduce the oven temperature to 375°F (190°C) and bake until the fruit is tender when pierced with a knife and the juices are bubbling, about 15 minutes. Remove the vanilla bean and serve the crumble hot or at room temperature.

Serve with a fresh, apricot-scented German Riesling.

COCONUT RICE PUDDING WITH PINEAPPLE IN CHILE SYRUP

The multicultural character of London has led to an astounding fusion of cuisines. In the kitchen of a large restaurant, Caribbean, Indian, Moroccan, Australian, New Zealand, Thai, African, and British chefs might be working alongside those from different European nationalities. As a result, flavoring an Anglo-Indian rice pudding with Caribbean rum and coconut and serving it with an Australian-influenced spiced pineapple compote seems natural. The combination is utterly delicious and strangely British.

1 To make the rice pudding, preheat the oven to 300°F (150°C). Generously butter a 4-cup (32–fl oz/ 1-l) baking dish.

2 In a bowl, stir together the brown sugar, rice, coconut, cinnamon, and salt. Transfer to the prepared dish. In the same bowl, stir together the milk, cream, and rum. Pour over the rice. Bake for 30 minutes. Remove from the oven, stir, reduce the oven temperature to 275°F (135°C), and bake, stirring occasionally, until the rice is meltingly tender and most of the liquid has been absorbed, about 1 hour.

3 Meanwhile, prepare the pineapple compote: In a small saucepan over medium heat, combine the granulated sugar, chile, star anise, cloves, and 1 cup (8 fl oz/250 ml) water. Bring to a boil, stirring occasionally, until the sugar is dissolved. Continue to cook until a thick syrup forms, about 10 minutes.

4 While the syrup is cooking, cut the green top off the pineapple, then cut a thin slice from the bottom. Stand the pineapple upright and, using a large, sharp knife, cut the peel away in vertical strips. Lay the pineapple on its side and align the blade with the diagonal rows of brown "eyes." Working in a spiral, cut at an angle on each side of the eyes to remove them. Cut the pineapple lengthwise into quarters. Remove the tough core from each quarter and then thinly slice crosswise. Place in a shallow nonreactive bowl. Pour the syrup over the pineapple and let cool to room temperature. Serve the pudding warm, at room temperature, or cold with the pineapple compote.

FOR THE RICE PUDDING

¾ cup (6 oz/185 g) firmly packed light brown sugar

⅓ cup (2 oz/60 g) Arborio rice

3 tablespoons unsweetened shredded coconut

½ teaspoon ground cinnamon

Pinch of fine sea salt

2¼ cups (18 fl oz/560 ml) whole milk

⅔ cup (5 fl oz/160 g) heavy (double) cream

3 tablespoons dark rum

FOR THE PINEAPPLE COMPOTE

½ cup (4 oz/125 g) granulated sugar

¼ red or green chile such as jalapeño, seeded and finely sliced

1 star anise

2 whole cloves

1 medium pineapple

Makes 4 servings

Mangoes

South American mangoes are sold in London throughout the year, but the true mango season begins in May. This is when the first crates of Alphonso mangoes from India and Pakistan arrive at the Great Western Market, just outside Heathrow Airport. The matte, yellow skin of this plump variety hides aromatic, nonfibrous, yellow flesh that is utterly delicious. They are packed six or twelve to a box, wrapped in crumpled paper with a few glittering strands of tinsel.

Boxes of Alphonso mangoes are stacked high in every Indian, Pakistani, and Middle Eastern grocery shop in the city. Canny shoppers carefully inspect the contents of each box. Ripe mangoes release a fragrance near their stem end and yield slightly to gentle pressure. Bruised, wrinkled, or very soft specimens are surreptitiously swapped for better fruits from other boxes before the shopper tries, often unsuccessfully, to bargain over the price. Once home, a whole box of mangoes can frequently be eaten in a few days. The season continues through June as other Indian varieties come on the market, such as honeyed Banganpali mangoes and sweet Kesar mangoes.

PEAR SOUFFLÉ

Dipping a spoon into an ethereal pear soufflé redolent of Poire William, the aromatic pear brandy, is sure to create a hush around the dinner table. In the 1950s and 1960s, every London debutante aspired to make a soufflé in a bid to woo a husband. The dessert fell out of favor but was reintroduced by Albert and Michel Roux from France, brothers and influential cutting-edge chefs who opened the Michelin-starred Le Gavroche in London in 1967, followed by Michel Roux's Waterside Inn in Berkshire. They are credited with creating the fashion for delicate fruit soufflés with a layer of macerated fruit in the center.

4 large ripe pears such as Comice, about 1½ lb (750 g) total weight

½ cup (4 oz/125 g) sugar, plus more for coating

Juice of 1 lemon

2 tablespoons arrowroot

4 tablespoons (2 fl oz/60 ml) Poire William

1 tablespoon unsalted butter, melted

4 large egg whites

Makes 8 servings

1 Peel and core 3 of the pears and coarsely dice. In a small nonreactive saucepan over medium-low heat, combine the diced pears, ½ cup sugar, and half of the lemon juice. Cook until the pears are meltingly soft and the sugar is dissolved, 15 minutes. Transfer to a food processor and purée until smooth. Return to the pan.

2 Place the arrowroot in a small bowl and slowly stir in 3 tablespoons of the Poire William until smooth. Using a wooden spoon, stir into the puréed pears. Bring to a boil over medium heat and cook, stirring constantly, until thickened, about 2 minutes. Remove from the heat and let cool for 1 hour.

3 Peel and core the remaining pear, then finely dice. Place in a bowl and stir in the remaining 1 tablespoon Poire William and the remaining lemon juice. Set aside for at least 20 minutes or up to 40 minutes.

4 Place a heavy baking sheet in the oven and preheat to 425°F (220°C). Brush eight ½-cup (4–fl oz/125-ml) ramekins with the melted butter and evenly coat with sugar to help the soufflés rise.

5 Strain the diced pears, reserving the liquid. Stir the liquid into the puréed pears. Put the egg whites in a large, clean bowl. Using a balloon whisk or an electric mixer on medium speed, beat until the whites begin to thicken. Continue to beat, increasing the speed to medium-high if using an electric mixer, just until soft, floppy peaks form. Using a metal spoon, fold one-third of the egg whites into the puréed pears to lighten. Gently fold in the remaining egg whites just until no white streaks remain.

6 Spoon the egg white mixture into the prepared ramekins to reach halfway up the sides. Sprinkle with the diced pears, dividing evenly. Top with the remaining egg white mixture. Tap each ramekin on a work surface to settle the contents. Place on the hot baking sheet, reduce the oven temperature to 350°F (180°C), and bake until well risen but slightly wobbly, about 10 minutes. Serve at once.

Serve with a late-harvest Chenin Blanc such as a Savennières or Montlouis.

MASALA CHAI ICE CREAM WITH SPICED BRANDY PRUNES

Masala chai is a deliciously sweet, milky Indian tea spiced with cardamom, cloves, and cinnamon. Like many traditional Indian preparations, it has begun to appear on the menus of some of London's top Michelin-starred Indian restaurants such as Zaika—not as a drink, but as a flavoring for dishes such as ice cream and rice pudding. Here, the subtly spiced tea is turned into a distinctive Western-style ice cream and paired with succulent prunes macerated in cinnamon and brandy. The longer the prunes are left to soak in the syrup, the more they will become imbued with the flavors of cinnamon and brandy.

1 To make the brandy prunes, cut the prunes in half and place in a small nonreactive saucepan with the Armagnac, sugar, cinnamon, and 2 tablespoons water. Set over low heat and cook, stirring occasionally, until the sugar is dissolved. Bring slowly to a boil, and as soon as the mixture bubbles, pour into a nonreactive bowl. Let cool to room temperature, then cover and macerate for 24 hours.

2 To make the ice cream, in a saucepan, combine the milk, cream, sugar, cardamom, cloves, and cinnamon. Set over low heat and warm the mixture just until small bubbles appear along the edge of the pan. Add the tea leaves, remove from the heat, and let stand to infuse the milk mixture for 10 minutes. Set over medium-low heat and heat until small bubbles form around the edge of the pan. Remove from the heat and let steep for 5 minutes longer. Strain through a fine-mesh sieve into a pitcher.

3 Place some ice and a little cold water in a large bowl. Set another bowl on top of the ice. Set aside. In a large bowl, whisk the egg yolks until smooth. Whisking constantly, slowly pour the hot milk mixture

into the egg yolks. Return to the saucepan, set over low heat, and cook, stirring constantly with a wooden spoon, until the custard thickens enough to coat the back of the spoon, 15–20 minutes. If you draw a finger down the back of the spoon, it should leave a line. Do not let the custard boil. Immediately strain the custard through a fine-mesh sieve into the bowl sitting on the ice. Stir until the custard cools.

4 Freeze in an ice-cream maker according to the manufacturer's directions. Transfer to an airtight container and place in the freezer.

5 To serve, place the ice cream in the refrigerator for 10 minutes to soften slightly. Scoop the ice cream into individual bowls. Spoon a few prunes and some their juice over each portion. Serve at once.

Note: The brandy prunes will keep up to 3 weeks stored in an airtight container in the refrigerator.

FOR THE BRANDY PRUNES

½ lb (250 g) large pitted prunes

⅔ cup (5 fl oz/160 ml) Armagnac brandy

3 tablespoons sugar

1 cinnamon stick, broken in half

FOR THE ICE CREAM

1 cup (8 fl oz/250 ml) whole milk

1¼ cups (10 fl oz/310 ml) heavy (double) cream

⅔ cup (5 oz/155 g) sugar

8 green cardamom pods, bruised

8 whole cloves

1 cinnamon stick, broken in half

2 tablespoons Assam tea leaves

6 large egg yolks

Makes 4 servings

GLOSSARY

ARMAGNAC A French brandy produced in the Gascony area and made from white grapes. The finest comes from the Bas-Armagnac region.

ARUGULA Also known as rocket, this peppery green has deeply notched leaves about 2 inches (5 cm) long. It is sold in bunches or as loose leaves.

ASIAN SESAME OIL Extracted from roasted sesame seeds, sesame oil is a fragrant, deep amber oil used primarily in Japan, Korea, and China, where it is preferred as a flavoring rather than a cooking oil.

ASSAM TEA A full-bodied black tea produced in the Assam region of India.

BELGIAN ENDIVE This torpedo-shaped member of the chicory family, also known as chicory or witloof, has a mildly bitter flavor and a crisp texture. The most common variety has yellow-tipped leaves; the rarer red-tipped type can be found in some markets. Refrigerate Belgian endive and use within a day after purchase to avoid bitterness.

BRIOCHE A soft, sweet French bread recognizable by its shape—a sort of fluted cupcake with a top-knot. Made in both small and large sizes, and occasionally as a rectangular loaf.

BUCKWHEAT FLOUR Dark flour made from the cereal-like seeds of the buckwheat plant. The flour has a nutty, slightly sweet flavor and a firm texture.

BULGUR Nutty-tasting, firm-textured bulgur, also known as bulghur or burghul, is made from wheat that has been steamed, dried, and cracked. It requires only brief preparation by cooking or soaking the grains. Sold in fine, medium, and coarse grinds.

BUTTER, CLARIFIED The liquid that separates from the milk solids of heated butter. It has a high smoke point that makes it excellent for frying.

MAKING CLARIFIED BUTTER: Melt 1 cup (8 oz/ 250 g) unsalted butter in a small saucepan over low heat. Simmer without stirring until the white milk solids settle in the pan bottom and start to turn golden, about 20 minutes. Skim any foam from the top of the melted butter. Remove from the heat, let cool slightly, and pour the clear liquid through a fine-mesh sieve into a glass container, leaving the white milk solids behind. Discard the solids. Cover and refrigerate for up to 3 months.

CANDIED CITRUS PEEL Citrus peel boiled and dipped in sugar is used in puddings, cakes, and breads. Candied peel is sold in specialty-food stores but can also be made at home.

MAKING CANDIED CITRUS PEEL: Remove the peels from 6–8 oranges or lemons in large pieces. Place in a saucepan with water to cover and boil for 1 minute. Drain, return to the pan with water to cover, and simmer 30 minutes. Let stand until the liquid reaches room temperature. Slice the peels into strips. Combine 1½ cups (12 oz/375 g) granulated sugar, ¼ cup (2 fl oz/60 g) light corn syrup, and 1½ cups (12 fl oz/375 ml) water in a saucepan, bring to a boil, and cook until the sugar dissolves and the syrup is clear. Add the peels and simmer until translucent, about 1 hour. Transfer to a rack set over a tray and let cool. Roll each strip in superfine (caster) sugar and return to the rack to dry for 1 hour. Coat the strips again and let dry for 1 hour. Store in an airtight container in the refrigerator, with superfine sugar sprinkled between each layer.

CELERY ROOT Related to celery, celery root has a similar but more pronounced flavor. Once the large brown bulb is peeled, the tender ivory flesh can be shredded and used raw in salads or cooked in much the same way as a potato. Also known as celeriac.

CHANTERELLE MUSHROOMS Trumpet-shaped mushrooms that are a bright golden yellow and have an earthy flavor with hints of apricot. This variety grows only in the wild and is not cultivated.

CHILES There are hundreds of chile varieties, from tiny to large and mild to fiery. To reduce the heat of fresh chiles, cut out the membranes and discard the seeds. When working with fresh chiles, avoid touching your eyes, mouth, or other sensitive areas. You can wear rubber gloves to protect your skin.

JALAPEÑO A bright green chile, about 1½ inches (4 cm) long, ranging from hot to very hot. Available canned or fresh and sometimes in its ripe, red state.

SERRANO A slender, shiny fresh red or green chile that is about 3 inches (7.5 cm) long and is very hot.

THAI OR BIRD A small, thin, extremely hot green or red fresh chile, usually about 1 inch (2.5 cm) long.

CHINESE RICE WINE To produce this full-bodied amber wine, glutinous rice and millet are fermented and aged for at least 10 years. It can be served as a beverage or used in cooking, primarily in marinades and sauces. The best rice wine is from eastern China and is named after the province of Shaoxing.

COINTREAU An orange-flavored liqueur used in drinks, desserts, and sauces. Other orange liqueurs, such as Grand Marnier, may be substituted.

CRÈME FRAÎCHE This cultured French cream is similar to sour cream, but will not separate when added to hot foods, and can be whipped. Look for it in the dairy section of markets, or make your own.

MAKING CRÈME FRAÎCHE: Stir 2 tablespoons buttermilk into 1 cup (8 fl oz/250 ml) heavy (double) cream in a plastic or glass container. Cover tightly and let stand in a warm spot, shaking once or twice, until thickened, 24–48 hours. Stir and use immediately, or cover and refrigerate for up to 1 week.

CREMINI MUSHROOMS Closely related to white button mushrooms, cremini mushrooms are about 1–2 inches (2.5–5 cm) in diameter and light brown in color and have a smooth round cap, firm texture, and full flavor. Large, fully mature cremini are known as portobello mushrooms. Some smaller cremini are labeled Baby Bellas.

CURRANTS, DRIED While fresh currants are berrylike fruits, dried currants are actually Zante grapes, tiny raisins with a distinctively tart-sweet flavor. If they are unavailable, substitute raisins.

CURRANTS, FRESH Grown in northern Europe and the United States, these black, red, or white berries are slightly tart and often sweetened before eaten. Fresh currants are in season from early July through early August and are often found in farmers' markets rather than supermarkets. Buy small, firm berries and refrigerate for no longer than 2 days.

FAVA BEANS Also called broad beans, these shell beans are available fresh in spring and early summer. The beans should be peeled of their tough outer skin unless they are very young and tender.

PEELING FAVA BEANS: Blanch the shelled beans briefly in boiling water, then immerse in ice water. Drain and pinch each bean to remove from the skin.

FERMENTED BLACK BEANS Sometimes called salted or preserved black beans, these pungent beans are soybeans that have been dried, salted, and allowed to ferment until they turn black. The beans should be rinsed gently in a fine-mesh sieve to remove excess salt before using in a recipe. They are sold in plastic bags and will keep for a year if stored in a cool, dry place.

GARAM MASALA A typical spice blend of northern India (*garam masala* means simply "spice blend") that generally includes black pepper, cardamom, cinnamon, cloves, coriander, cumin, dried chiles, fennel, mace, and nutmeg. For optimal freshness, store the blend in a cool, dry place for no longer than 6 months.

GELATIN Made from animal protein, gelatin is a colorless, flavorless thickener available as fine granules and in sheets. To use, soften it, without stirring, in cold liquid, then stir thoroughly into the liquid to be jelled and heat it gently without allowing it to boil. When cooled, the mixture will set into a firm mass.

GLACÉ CHERRIES These candied cherries are used chiefly in breads, cakes, and puddings. Look for them in gourmet food shops and store in an airtight container in a cool, dry place. Dried cherries can be substituted but will alter the texture and taste of the final product.

GOLDEN SYRUP A clear, golden liquid sweetener made from refined cane sugar. It is popular in England, where it is used as a topping and spread, as an ingredient in cake and dessert recipes, or as a substitute for corn syrup. Lyle's is the most popular and available brand.

GREEK YOGURT Made from cow's or sheep's milk, Greek yogurt is thicker and less sour than other types of yogurts. If Greek yogurt is unavailable, place plain whole-milk yogurt in a colander lined with cheesecloth (muslin) set over a bowl and let drain overnight in the refrigerator.

GREEN CARDAMOM PODS Belonging to the ginger family, the cardamom plant bears pods containing seeds that have a spicy, aromatic flavor. Green cardamom has the most delicate flavor and is the most popular type. When ground, the seeds give off a camphorlike aroma, although the taste is sweet and mild. For the freshest results, buy whole pods and remove and grind the seeds as needed.

HADDOCK, SMOKED AND FRESH Mild-flavored and lean white-fleshed fish harvested from the Atlantic Ocean. Haddock can be cooked by most methods, except on the grill, where it may flake. Cod, with its similar taste and texture, can be used interchangeably with haddock. Finnan haddock, or finnan haddie, is a type of smoked haddock from Scotland that is popular in Britain.

HORSERADISH Native to Europe and Asia, this gnarled root has a pungent flavor that contributes a spicy bite to sauces and side dishes and pairs well with roast beef. Look for fresh horseradish in produce markets. If it is unavailable, you can substitute bottled, or prepared, horseradish, which is grated and mixed with vinegar.

LEMONGRASS This long, slender, fibrous, lemon-scented grass native to Asia is a staple flavoring in many Asian cuisines. The bulbous base is either pounded or thinly sliced to release its fragrance. The coarse upper portion is discarded. If fresh lemongrass is unavailable, substitute 1 tablespoon slivered lemon balm or chopped lemon zest. Lemongrass will keep for up to 2 weeks in the refrigerator.

MANDARIN PEEL, DRIED The dried peels of mandarins are used as a flavoring in many Chinese dishes. They are often ground, and sold in Asian markets and farmers' markets. Dried tangerine peel or orange peel can be substituted.

MEDJOOL DATES Classified as soft dates, Medjool dates have a high moisture content and soft texture. Although their dry, sticky exterior suggests that they are dried fruits, most dates are sold fresh. They should be tightly wrapped in plastic and will keep in the refrigerator for up to 3 weeks after purchase.

OYSTER SAUCE A concentrated dark brown sauce made from dried oysters, salt, water, cornstarch (cornflour), and caramel. The slightly sweet, smoky-flavored sauce originated in southern China. The least expensive products lack a rich oyster flavor and should be avoided. Once opened, oyster sauce should be stored in the refrigerator.

PHEASANT Native to Asia and also found in Europe and North America, pheasant is a medium-sized game bird. Farm-raised birds have a less pronounced gamy flavor than wild pheasants, and females tend to be plumper and more tender than males. Whole pheasants, weighing 2–3 pounds (1–1.5 kg), or parts such as breasts may be ordered from meat markets. They are also sold frozen in some specialty-food stores.

POIRE WILLIAM Fruit brandies, or eaux-de-vie, are distilled liquors produced from a variety of fruits. The most common brandy is made with grapes. Poire William is derived from pears, framboise from raspberries, kirsch from cherries, and calvados from apples. These brandies are not sweet but are imbued with the intense fragrance and flavor of the fruit from which they are made. It often takes as many as 18 pounds (9 kg) of fruit to produce a small bottle of eau-de-vie.

POMEGRANATE MOLASSES This thick syrup is made from reduced pomegranate juice. The final product is not strictly molasses, but the term refers to the liquid's thick, syrupy texture. Long a staple in Middle Eastern cooking, pomegranate molasses is being increasingly used in the West in sauces, soups, and salad dressings. It is available in most Middle Eastern markets and gourmet food stores.

PROSCIUTTO Italian ham that is seasoned, salt-cured, and air-dried. Its distinctive fragrance and subtle flavor make prosciutto one of the world's favorite hams. Prosciutto from Parma, Italy, which is aged from 10 months to 2 years, is considered among the best.

QUAIL EGGS Although much smaller than chicken eggs, quail eggs have a similar flavor and texture. With shells speckled in color from dark brown to blue and white, they are attractive to serve hard-boiled in the shell as an hors d'oeuvre, a garnish, or an accompaniment for salads. Five quail eggs are equivalent to one chicken egg.

QUINCE A relative of the rose, the quince resembles a misshapen yellow apple. The hard, dry flesh has an intensely astringent flavor when raw. Once cooked, however, the flesh becomes a deep rose pink and gains a heady fragrance. Quinces are available October through December in farmers' markets and specialty-food stores. Unripe fruits should be stored at cool room temperature for up to 1 month. Ripe quinces should be kept in a plastic bag in the refrigerator for up to 2 weeks.

RHUBARB Long, celery-like stalks that are very sour when raw but gain a soft texture and appealing tartness when cooked with sugar in desserts such as pies and tarts; jams, preserves, chutneys; and sauces for savory dishes. The stalks range in color from bright red to pink streaked with pale green. The leaves contain oxalic acid, a potentially toxic substance, and should be removed. Hothouse-grown rhubarb is available year-round in some areas; field-grown rhubarb reaches markets in April and May.

ROSE WATER Derived from a distillation of rose petals, rose water has an intensely aromatic flavor and fragrance. It has been used for centuries as a flavoring in Middle Eastern, Indian, and English cuisines. Rose water is available in gourmet food stores and Middle Eastern markets.

SCALLOPS The flesh of these popular bivalves has a smooth texture and an appealing sweetness. In the United States, scallops are usually shucked before they are sold. Occasionally in American markets and generally in European ones, scallops are found in their shells. Purchase scallops the day you plan to serve them and refrigerate until ready to use.

BAY The most highly regarded scallop, harvested from a small region of the Atlantic Ocean. The little morsels, about ½ inch (12 mm) in diameter, have a sweet, delicate flavor.

SEA The most common type of scallop. At about 1½ inches (4 cm) in diameter, they are larger than bay scallops and not quite as tender. Check for freshness when purchasing, as fishing boats often stay out on the ocean for weeks at a time.

SORREL A long, narrow leaf appreciated for its highly acidic, tart, almost lemony flavor. The delicate leaves have the unusual ability to melt into a purée when exposed to heat and are a popular source of flavoring in sauces, soups, and stuffings. Very young leaves are used raw in salads.

SOY SAUCE, NATURALLY BREWED A ubiquitous Asian seasoning, made from fermented soybean meal and wheat. Naturally brewed soy sauce has a full-bodied taste and is superior to the synthetic versions containing sweeteners and coloring agents.

SPANISH CHORIZO SAUSAGE Made with dried pork and heavily spiced with garlic and paprika, chorizo sausage has a rich, smoky-sweet flavor with a hint of tanginess. Sausages from Spain tend not to be as spicy-hot as Mexican-style chorizo, but the latter may be used as a substitute.

STAR ANISE The star-shaped pod, or fruit, borne by a small evergreen tree of the magnolia family. The seed-bearing pods are picked when they are unripe and then are dried. Their flavor and aroma are sweet, strong, and licorice-like. Despite the name, star anise is unrelated to anise.

TAHINI This paste made from ground sesame seeds has a rich, creamy flavor and a concentrated sesame taste. Tahini is an essential ingredient in hummus, baba ghanoush, and other Middle Eastern dishes. Be sure to stir before using, as the oil often separates from the paste.

THAI FISH SAUCE A thin, clear liquid made from salted and fermented fish and ranging in color from amber to dark brown. It has a pungent aroma and a strong, salty flavor. Southeast Asians use fish sauce in the same way that Westerners use salt, both as a cooking seasoning and at the table. Bottles of Thai fish sauce are often labeled *nam pla*.

TOMATOES Round, plum, and cherry are the three basic types of tomatoes. Medium or large round tomatoes are excellent for slicing, while egg-shaped plum, or Roma, tomatoes have more pulp and less juice, making them ideal for sauces. Small cherry tomatoes are available in a variety of colors.

PEELING AND SEEDING TOMATOES: Cut a shallow X in the blossom end of each tomato. Immerse in a pan of boiling water until the peel begins to curl away from the X, about 30 seconds. Transfer to a bowl of ice water to cool, then peel away the skin. To seed, cut in half crosswise and squeeze each half gently to dislodge the seeds.

TURMERIC A ground spice in the ginger family that is valued for its earthy flavor and its intense yellow-orange color. Widely grown and processed in India, turmeric is the main ingredient in commercial curry powder. Fresh turmeric, which resembles fresh ginger, is also used in Asian cuisines.

INDEX

Potatoes
    bangers and mash, 128
    fish and chips, 127
    fish pie, 147
    and pea samosas, 96
    vegetable crisps, 91
    watercress soup, 109
Prosciutto
    about, 186
    arugula salad with quince cheese and, 118
Prunes, spiced brandy, 183
Pubs, 18, 50, 52
Pudding, meaning of, 157

Q

Quail eggs
    about, 186
    salad, sorrel, lettuce, and, 114
Quince
    about, 186
    cheese, arugula salad with prosciutto and, 118

R

Raita, 152
Raspberries
    and peach trifle, 163
    summer pudding, 160
Restaurants
    ethnic, 16, 17, 18
    history of, 11, 13
    by neighborhood, 25–27
    trendsetting, 16, 17
    upscale, 18
Rhubarb
    about, 187
    fool, 171
Rice pudding, coconut, with pineapple, 179
Rice wine, Chinese, 185
Rose water, 187

S

Salads
    arugula, with quince cheese and prosciutto, 118
    Asian grilled salmon, 117
    Belgian endive, pear, feta, and walnut, 110
    chickpea, tomato, and chorizo, 105
    crab, avocado, and watercress, spicy, 106
    sorrel, lettuce, and quail egg, 114

Salmon
    salad, Asian grilled, 117
    smoked, 143
    smoked, blini with crème fraîche and, 87
Samosas, pea and potato, 96
Sandwiches
    bacon and egg butties, 139
    egg and cress, 75
    finger, 34
    history of, 75
Sausage
    bangers and mash, 128
    chorizo, 187
    chorizo, chickpea, and tomato salad, 105
Scallops
    about, 187
    fish pie, 147
    seared, with tagliatelle, fava beans,
        and bacon, 144
Scones
    about, 35
    cheese and ham, 76
Sea bass, steamed, with ginger
    and black beans, 148
Sesame oil, Asian, 185
Shrimp
    brown, 56
    fish pie, 147
    potted, 88
Sole, Dover, 57
Sorrel
    about, 187
    salad, lettuce, quail egg, and, 114
Soufflé, pear, 180
Soups
    cucumber, chilled, 113
    pea, 121
    watercress, 109
Soy sauce, 187
Spinach, seared duck breasts with, 132
Star anise, 187
Strawberries
    about, 167
    pain perdu, 167
    summer pudding, 160
Summer pudding, 160

T

Tahini, 187

Tarts
    Stilton and leek, 95
    treacle, 164
Tea. *See also* Afternoon tea
    brewing, 39
    coffee vs., 40, 79
    history of, 36
    masala chai ice cream, 183
    merchants, 36
    museum, 38
    serving, 39
    varieties of, 39, 40–41, 185
Toffee pudding, sticky, 172
Tomatoes
    chicken tikka masala, 151
    Mediterranean meze plate, 99
    peeling and seeding, 187
    salad, chickpea, chorizo, and, 105
    varieties of, 187
Treacle tart, 164
Trifle, peach and raspberry, 163
Turmeric, 187

V

Vegetables. *See also individual vegetables*
    crisps, 91
    Mediterranean meze plate, 99
Venison with red wine jus and roasted parsnips, 131
Victoria sponge, 34
Vodka espresso, 61

W

Walnuts
    and coffee cake, 35
    salad, Belgian endive, pear, feta, and, 110
Watercress
    and egg sandwiches, 75
    salad, spicy crab, avocado, and, 106
    soup, 109
Wine
    Champagne cocktail, 61
    Chinese rice, 185
    merchants, 131

Y

Yogurt
    Greek, 186
    raita, 152
Yorkshire pudding, 140

ACKNOWLEDGMENTS

Sybil Kapoor would like to thank Raj Kapoor, Lorna Wing, Louise Mackaness, Jean-Blaise Hall, Rosemary Scoular, Sophie Laurimore, Caroline Stacey, Jonathan Downey, Susan Low, Gerhard Jenne, Vineet Bhatia, Nino Sassu, Randolph Hodgson, Patricia Michelson, Nick Strangeway, Harriet Docker, Lindsay Stewart, and Peter Haydon for all their help, as well as the many other Londoners who gladly supplied information whenever it was needed. She would also like to thank the team at Weldon Owen, including Hannah Rahill, Kim Goodfriend, and Nicky Collings.

Weldon Owen and the photography team would like to give an especially big thank-you to the fabulous employees and owners of Assaggi, Bramah Museum of Tea and Coffee, Cecconi's, Club Gascon, Fergus Henderson and the employees of St John Bar and Restaurant and St John Bread & Wine (and for the best Eccles cake we've ever tasted); John Duffell and Steve Duffell of Cranleigh Fishmongers; Ken and Maria (Mum) Collings; Le Truc Vert; No. 6 George Street Restaurant and Shop; E&O (especially our favorite bartender!); Rasoi Vineet Bhatia; Sandra Hanauer for her beautiful cakes and other teatime treats; The Jerusalem Tavern; The Westbourne Pub; West Cornwall Pasty Co., and the local farmers' markets, seafood and meat markets, street markets, and covered markets of London. They also wish to extend their gratitude to the owners and workers of the restaurants, bakeries, shops, and other culinary businesses in London who participated in this project: & Clarke's, A. Gold, Baker & Spice, Berry Bros. & Rudd, Books for Cooks, Café des Amis Wine Bar, Camisa & Son, Chalmers & Gray, C. Lidgate Butcher and Charcutier, Charbonnel et Walker, Churchill Arms, Coach & Horses, Costas Fish Restaurants, Fifteen, Floridita, Fortnum & Mason, Fresh & Wild, Gerry's Wine and Spirits, Golborne Fisheries, Gordon Ramsay at Claridge's, Hakkasan, Harrod's, Konditor & Cook, L'Artisan du Chocolat, La Fromagerie, Lamb & Flag, Le Gavroche, Lina Stores, London Chocolate Society, Masters Super Fish, Match Bar, Moro, Neal's Yard Dairy, Patisserie Valerie, Paxton and Whitfield, Rococo Chocolates, Sketch, Speck, Talad Thai, Tamarind, The Eagle Pub, The Fish Shop, The George Inn, The Ginger Pig, The Oak, The Palm Court at The Ritz, The Pie Man, The River Café, The Townhouse, Vama, Yauatcha, Zafferano, and Zuma. For the beautiful props, a special thank-you to Summerill & Bishop, including owners Bernadette, June, and Aurolie, and to The Conran Shop. The team would also like to thank Garibaldi's and Pacific Coast Brewing Co. in Oakland, California, and Elite Café in San Francisco, California.

Weldon Owen also wishes to thank the following individuals for their kind assistance: Desne Ahlers, Ken DellaPenta, Judith Dunham, Carolyn R. Keating, Denise Santoro Lincoln, and Lorna Wing.

PHOTO CREDITS
Jean-Blaise Hall, all photography, except for the following:
Francesca Yorke: Front cover (bottom), Pages 52 (bottom), 92, 116, 128, 133, 136, 139, 147, 149, 160, 162, 176
Martin Brigdale: Pages 72, 121, 134, 143, 152, 181, 183

PHOTOGRAPHY LOCATIONS

The following London locations have been given references for the map on pages 28–29.

OXMOOR HOUSE INC.

Oxmoor House books are distributed by Sunset Books
80 Willow Road, Menlo Park, CA 94025
Telephone: 650-321-3600 Fax: 650-324-1532
Vice President/General Manager Rich Smeby
National Accounts Manager/Special Sales Brad Moses
Oxmoor House and Sunset Books are divisions of
Southern Progress Corporation

WILLIAMS-SONOMA, INC.

Founder & Vice-Chairman Chuck Williams

THE FOODS OF THE WORLD SERIES

Conceived and produced by Weldon Owen Inc.
814 Montgomery Street, San Francisco, CA 94133
Telephone: 415-291-0100 Fax: 415-291-8841

In Collaboration with Williams-Sonoma, Inc.
3250 Van Ness Avenue, San Francisco, CA 94109

A Weldon Owen Production
Copyright © 2005 Weldon Owen Inc.
and Williams-Sonoma, Inc.

First printed in 2005
10 9 8 7 6 5 4 3 2 1

ISBN 0-8487-3102-6

Printed by Tien Wah Press
Printed in Singapore

WELDON OWEN INC.

Chief Executive Officer John Owen
President and Chief Operating Officer Terry Newell
Chief Financial Officer Christine E. Munson
Vice President International Sales Stuart Laurence
Creative Director Gaye Allen
Publisher Hannah Rahill

Series Editor Kim Goodfriend
Editorial Assistant Juli Vendzules

Art Director Nicky Collings
Senior Designer Alison Fenton
Designer Rachel Lopez

Production Director Chris Hemesath
Color Specialist Teri Bell
Production and Reprint Coordinator Todd Rechner

Food Stylists Louise Mackaness, George Dolese
Food Stylist's Assistants Chrissy Schmidt,
Elisabet der Nederlanden
Prop Stylists Harriet Docker, George Dolese
Photographer's Assistant Nigel James
Map Illustrator Bart Wright

JACKET IMAGES

Front cover: London Parliament; Steak, Mushroom,
and Ale Pie, page 136, with mashed potatoes. Back
cover: sausage man at Borough Market, pouring tea,
pork pies at Borough Market. Front flap: Portobello
Market. Back flap: London taxicabs on Victoria Street.

A NOTE ON WEIGHTS AND MEASURES

All recipes include customary U.S. and metric
measurements. Metric conversions are based on
a standard developed for these books and have
been rounded off. Actual weights may vary.